£16·50

POLICY AND PRACTICE IN EDUCATION

SPECIAL EDUCATIONAL NEEDS:
PROVIDING ADDITIONAL SUPPORT

Second Edition

POLICY AND PRACTICE IN EDUCATION

POLICY AND PRACTICE IN EDUCATION

SERIES EDITORS
JIM O'BRIEN and CHRISTINE FORDE

SPECIAL EDUCATIONAL NEEDS: PROVIDING ADDITIONAL SUPPORT

Second Edition

Sheila Riddell

*Professor of Inclusion and Diversity
at the Moray House School of Education
University of Edinburgh*

DUNEDIN ACADEMIC PRESS
EDINBURGH

3230316216
IAGPS489
(371.9094)
RID

Published by
Dunedin Academic Press Ltd
Hudson House
8 Albany Street
Edinburgh EH1 3QB
Scotland

ISBN 1 903765 70 6
ISBN 13: 978-1-903765-70-8
ISSN 1479-6910

First Edition 2002
Second Edition 2006

British Library Cataloguing in Publication Data
A catalogue record for this book is available from the British Library

Typeset by Makar Publishing Production
Printed in Great Britain by Cromwell Press

CONTENTS

v

SERIES EDITORS' INTRODUCTION

The area of special education remains a central concern in Scottish education but as attitudes and sensibilities have evolved so too has policy and practice. A second edition of *Special Educational Needs: Providing Additional Support* is, therefore, timely. In Scotland the recent legislation in relation to 'additional support needs' as well as a number of policy initiatives including the report *Better Behaviour – Better Learning* and the ongoing development of a *Curriculum for Excellence* all raise significant questions for teachers and schools as they take forward the inclusion agenda. The author provides an updated, comprehensive account of special education in Scotland dealing with questions of significance for schools, teachers, pupils and their parents.

Sheila Riddell guides us through the range of significant issues by mapping out the changing nature of educational provision in this area. The historical context helps us appreciate that effective and high quality provision for all pupils is both an educational concern and a matter of social justice. Consequently, schools and teachers are often faced with significant dilemmas when trying to balance different educational needs. Providing for the education of all children and young people is making new demands on schools. Drawing from research, Sheila Riddell appraises current practices critically, pointing up many of the tensions and, indeed, dilemmas schools face as they have to address increasingly diverse and sometimes competing range of needs. More fundamentally, this book challenges current perceptions about inclusion.

Dr Jim O'Brien
Vice Dean and Director,
Centre for Educational Leadership,
Faculty of Education,
Moray House School of Education,
The University of Edinburgh

Dr Christine Forde
Senior Lecturer in Educational Studies
The University of Glasgow

ACKNOWLEDGEMENTS

This book refers to a number of research projects in which I have been involved over recent years. Chapters 2 and 3 draw on data from the Economic and Social Research Council (ESRC) funded project *The Justice Inherent in Special Educational Needs Assessments in England and Scotland*. My collaborators on this project were Professor Michael Adler and Dr Enid Mordaunt of the University of Edinburgh and Alastair Wilson of the Strathclyde Centre for Disability Research, University of Glasgow. Chapter 5 draws on data from the research project *Raising the Attainment of Pupils with Special Educational Needs* funded by the Scottish Executive Education Department. I collaborated on this project with Pauline Banks and Alastair Wilson of the Strathclyde Centre for Disability Research, University of Glasgow, Jean Kane of the St Andrew's Faculty of Education, University of Glasgow and Professor Alan Dyson, Dr Alan Millward and Anne Baynes of the Special Educational Needs Research Centre, University of Newcastle. I would like to thank all of these people for their contribution to the development of my thinking about disability and education. The interpretation of data in these chapters is my own. Finally, I would like to thank Ken, Annie and Bella for their constant love and support.

Chapter 1

INTRODUCTION: THE HISTORICAL CONTEXT

Introduction: the purpose and focus of the book

Education for children with additional support needs is an area of great importance not just for 'special education' professionals, but also for parents, children and young people and all those who have an interest in the broad field of education. Exploring the way in which mainstream education policies are experienced by those at the margins provides insights into the limitations or unintended consequences of these policies. Similarly, considering the type of provision made for disabled children and young people reveals a great deal about wider social values and priorities. This book explores the development of additional support needs policies and practices from the eighteenth century to the present and the ways in which these are experienced at grass roots level by key players. Where appropriate, comparisons are made with policy and practice in England, since contrasting Scottish experience with that of other parts of the UK throws Scottish experience into relief and provides insight into the distinctiveness of the Scottish tradition.

The focus of the book is on additional support needs policy as it applies to children. There have also been important developments in policy and practice for young people in the post-16 age group. These are referred to, but the scope of the book does not allow for detailed discussion. The structure of the book is as follows. Chapter 1 provides a brief summary of the development of special educational needs (SEN) policy and practice from the eighteenth century to the reports of the Warnock Committee (DES, 1978) and of the Scottish HMI (SED, 1978). This chapter explores the twin elements at play in provision for children with additional support needs. On the one hand, there has always been a desire to separate out children identified as different from others, emphasising distinctions between groups based on deficits. On the other hand, there has been a growing sense of social obligation to children with additional support needs, accompanied by the recognition that, if they are to make progress, additional resources have to be committed to their education. From the earliest times tensions can be discerned between social inclusion and human capital imperatives. The former suggests that the main purpose of education is to create social cohesion and

1

develop shared norms and values, whilst the latter suggests that the rationale for state education is to contribute to the generation of wealth, with greatest investment being made in those who are likely to provide the best financial returns. The Labour–Liberal coalition government in Scotland has emphasised social justice and the need to build social capital, but nonetheless human capital imperatives tend to be prioritised.

In Chapter 2, we consider recent developments in Scottish education policy for children and young people with SEN, making comparisons with English policy. Using a framework developed by Kirp (1982), it is argued that additional support needs policy in Scotland continues to be informed principally by the traditional frameworks of bureaucracy and professionalism, whereas English policy has been shaped by a wider range of policies including managerialism, marketisation, consumerism and legality. Recent legislative developments in Scotland have attempted to introduce a more eclectic policy mix, but nonetheless the traditional policy frameworks of professionalism and bureaucracy continue to hold sway north of the Border. In Chapter 3, using four case study local authorities in Scotland and England, we discuss the way in which the different national frameworks were experienced in specific local contexts. It is evident that whilst national policies may look quite different in the abstract, when they are applied in real social settings they are transformed and subverted by the key players. Scottish policy has tended to deliver less power to the service consumer, whereas English policy, at least on paper, allows consumers a greater role. In practice, in both England and Scotland, socio-economic status has had a major influence on parents' level of involvement and, particularly for socially-disadvantaged families, may override attempts at consumer empowerment south of the Border.

In Chapter 4, the meaning of inclusion and links with the wider social inclusion policy framework are outlined. Different understandings of inclusion and debates between 'integrationists' and 'inclusionists' are explored. Data are presented on the placement of children with additional support needs in mainstream and special schools and units. Given the current emphasis on evidence-based policy, we consider what evidence would be needed to determine whether progress towards inclusion is taking place. Given the growth in the number of special units and the decline in the number of special schools, we suggest that it is very difficult to know whether inclusion policies are being successful, or are producing different forms of exclusion. We also consider recent efforts to enhance the inclusion of children with social, emotional and behavioural difficulties through the *Better Behaviour – Better Learning* initiative (Scottish Executive, 2001a) and the possible future impact of developments within the *Curriculum for Excellence* programme.

Chapter 5 focuses on the tension between social inclusion and raising attainment policies, both of which have formed a key part of New Labour's educational agenda. In line with social inclusion goals, it was decided to include children with SEN in the target-setting programme. The performance of most schools is measured in relation to children's performance in national tests and Scottish Qualifications Agency examinations. However, there has always been confusion about whether the performance of children with additional support needs should be included in the reporting of outcomes. Excluding children with SEN implies that their performance cannot be measured or is less relevant to assessing overall quality. Including them in overall judgements of a mainstream school's performance, however, may create perverse incentives, encouraging exclusion rather than inclusion. A solution promoted by the Scottish Executive is to assess the performance of children with additional support needs in terms of their attainment of long- and short-term targets specified within an Individualised Educational Programme (IEP). Drawing on evidence from a Scottish Executive funded project, this chapter considers the strengths and weaknesses of the target-setting initiative in relation to children with additional support needs and the implications for combining accountability and inclusion agendas.

Finally, Chapter 6 discusses the content and implications of the Special Educational Needs and Disability Act 2001, which amended Part 4 of the Disability Discrimination Act, and was implemented from September 2002. Since equality is a reserved matter, this legislation covered Scotland, England and Wales, although it was implemented through separate national educational frameworks. The form which the legislation finally took and the complexities of trying to apply common UK policies through different national legislative frameworks, are discussed. The wider implications of basing educational provision for children with additional support needs on rights rather than needs and the future implications of the legislation are considered. It is argued that, relative to the future impact of the Education (Additional Support for Learning) (Scotland) Act 2004, the effect of the disability rights legislation may be fairly restricted.

A note on terminology

Following the passage of the additional support for learning legislation in Scotland, the term 'special educational needs', used in the Warnock Report, was replaced by the term 'additional support needs', encapsulating all children requiring extra support to make progress in education for whatever reasons. In this book, when referring to recent developments in the field, the term 'additional support needs' is used. However, when referring to earlier policy, practice and research, the term 'special educational needs' is used, because this was the language in currency at the time. It is also used in relation to policy and practice in the rest of the UK and in the US.

Provision for children with special educational needs: early developments

The following paragraphs draw on reviews of historical developments undertaken by Tomlinson (1982) and the report of the Warnock Committee (DES, 1978). Educational provision for disabled children has been in existence for only a relatively short period of time. Establishments catering for children with sensory impairments were the first to emerge. In 1793, the Asylum for the Industrious Blind was founded in Edinburgh. Funded by social philanthropists, its aim was to provide vocational training for future employment, and it relied upon profits from workshops to cover its running costs. The first school for the deaf in Great Britain was opened by Thomas Braidwood in Edinburgh in the early 1760s. Mr Braidwood's Academy for the Deaf and Dumb (these two categories were regarded as indistinguishable) catered for a small number of fee-paying pupils. In 1783, the Academy moved to London where, in 1792, the first English school for the deaf opened with six children under the direction of Braidwood's nephew. Other Braidwood schools subsequently opened in major cities. Donaldson's Hospital (now school) for the Deaf in Edinburgh was opened in 1850.

Education for children with learning difficulties was slower to emerge. A school for the education of 'imbeciles' was established at Baldovan in Dundee in 1852; it later became Strathmartine Hospital. An institution for 'defectives' was established in Edinburgh, moving to a site in Larbert in 1863, where it was renamed the Royal National Scottish Hospital. The Lunacy (Scotland) Act of 1862 recognised the needs of the 'mentally handicapped' and authorised the granting of licenses to charitable institutions established for the care and training of 'imbecile' children.

Developments between 1872 and 1945

The Education (Scotland) Act 1872 established school boards to provide elementary education in those areas where there were insufficient places in voluntary schools. The Act did not specifically include disabled children among those for whom provision was to be made. However, by 1874, 50 blind children were being educated in mainstream schools alongside their peers. Disabled children who could be accommodated in mainstream schools would receive some education, but others who could not be accommodated would receive no schooling at all.

The lack of provision for such children caused increasing concern and in 1886 the Royal Commission on the Blind and Deaf was set up, chaired by Lord Egerton, an aristocrat with interests in the West Indian sugar business. The Commission report of 1889 concluded that: 'It is better for the state to expend its funds on the elementary technical education of the blind, than to have to support them through life in idleness.' The report underlined the economic arguments for educating disabled children and young people:

The blind, deaf, dumb and the educable class of imbecile . . . if left uneducated, become not only a burden to themselves but a weighty burden on the state. It is in the interests of the state to educate them, so as to dry up, as far as possible, the minor streams which must ultimately swell to a great torrent of pauperism. (Egerton Commission, 1889)

In Scotland, legislation swiftly followed the report's publication. The Education of Blind and Deaf Mute Children (Scotland) Act of 1890 required authorities to make provision, in their own or other schools, for the education of blind and deaf children resident in their area who were not otherwise receiving suitable elementary education. Education for these children was to extend to the age of 16, much later than other children who might be given total or partial exemption from the age of 11.

The Egerton Commission's Report distinguished between idiots, imbeciles and the feeble-minded. Whereas 'idiots' were regarded as ineducable and therefore should be retained in asylums or workhouses, it was believed that 'imbeciles', and 'the feeble-minded' could be taught basic tasks. In Scotland, the Education of Defective Children (Scotland) Act of 1906 empowered school boards to make provision in special schools or classes for the education of defective children between the ages of 5 and 16. It is interesting to reflect on the time lag between education for children with sensory impairments and those with cognitive difficulties. This is probably due to the fact that during the nineteenth century many children would be uneducated and illiterate. The gap between those with learning difficulties and others would therefore be much less marked.

The Mental Deficiency (Scotland) Act of 1913 required school boards to ascertain children in their area who were defective. Those who were considered incapable of benefiting from instruction in special schools were to be placed in an institution. This system of ascertainment quickly came to be regarded as stigmatising and many parents refused to present their children for assessment. In 1924, the Mental Deficiency Committee (the Wood Committee) recommended that there should be a closer association between special and mainstream schools and that special schools 'should be presented to parents not as something both distinct and humiliating, but as a helpful variation of the ordinary school'. By 1939, the number of mentally defective children on the roll of special schools and classes had reached 4,871.

The development of child guidance services

During the first half of the twentieth century, there was a growing interest in psychometric testing to measure intelligence and to identify psychological problems. In Scotland in the late 1920s, an 'educational' clinic was opened by Dr William Boyd of the Education Department of the University of Glasgow and a 'psychological' clinic was established by Professor James Drever in the Psychology Department at Edinburgh University. The term 'child guidance clinic' was first used when the Notre Dame Clinic was opened in Glasgow. In 1937, Glasgow was the first education authority to establish a child guidance clinic on a full-time basis.

Developments between 1945 and 1978

The Education (Scotland) Act 1945 placed a general duty on education authorities to provide education for children which was suitable to their 'age, aptitude and ability'. In addition, there was a specific duty to establish which children, as a result of 'disability of mind or body', required 'special educational treatment' at school, including junior occupational centres, and which children were too handicapped to benefit from any form of education or training. To achieve this, parents could be required to submit their children for a medical examination (from 1969, extended to a psychological examination as well). Parents could appeal against a medical certificate which showed their child required special educational treatment and to the Sheriff Court against being refused permission to withdraw their child from a special school. Education authorities were empowered (after 1969 required) to provide child guidance services and to provide 'special educational treatment'.

Regulations issued in 1954 defined the following nine legal categories of 'handicap' for which special educational provision should be made: deafness, partial deafness, blindness, partial sightedness, mental handicap, epilepsy, speech defects, maladjustment and physical handicap. The categories did not include children with milder learning difficulties, nor those whose difficulties stemmed from such factors as absenteeism or frequent change of school. The Schools (Scotland) Code 1956 laid down maximum class sizes for the various categories of handicap so as to ensure that pupils in special schools got more individual attention. There continued to be some ambivalence about how many children were to be given 'special educational treatment'. The Scottish Education Department in a 1955 circular indicated that it did not envisage a large-scale system of separate special schools:

> It is recognised that there must continue to be situations where it is essential in children's interests that the handicapped must be separated from those who are not. Nevertheless as medical knowledge increases and as general school conditions improve it should be possible for an increasing proportion of pupils who require special educational treatment to be educated along with their contemporaries in ordinary schools. Special educational treatment should be regarded simply as a well-defined arrangement within the ordinary educational

system to provide for the handicapped child the individual attention that he particularly needs. (SED Circular 3000, 1955, para 4)

Arguably, this circular reflects similar assumptions to those underpinning the Education (Standards in Scotland's Schools etc.) (Scotland) Act 2000, which establishes the presumption that a child will be placed in a mainstream school unless there are particular reasons for choosing a special school placement. Educational services were particularly slow to develop for 'maladjusted' children. The development of child guidance clinics focused more attention on their needs and from 1933, approved schools had catered for children and young people who were ordered to be sent there by the courts. These schools provided a general education, with considerable emphasis on the development of vocational skills, and also focused on social readjustment. In 1971, all the functions of the approved schools, including the provision of education, were transferred to local authority social work departments under the terms of the Social Work (Scotland) Act 1968. The institutions were renamed List D schools.

Children with profound and complex learning difficulties were also poorly educated. From 1947, children described as 'ineducable but trainable' were placed in junior occupational centres where they were trained by instructors. Following the Report of the Melville Committee and the provisions of the Education (Mentally Handicapped Children) (Scotland) Act 1974, the centres were renamed schools and teachers were appointed in addition to instructors. The 1974 Act also gave local authorities responsibility for the education of children described as 'ineducable and untrainable'.

The Warnock and HMI reports of 1978

The Warnock Report (DES, 1978) has been seen as a watershed in thinking about provision for disabled children. Before 1978, children were 'ascertained' by medical officers as in need of 'special educational treatment' if they were deemed to fit into one of the nine legal categories of 'handicap' described above. There was growing dissatisfaction with the medical view of a fixed 'disability of mind and body' and the Warnock Report suggested a new and all-embracing category of 'special educational needs' to replace the former statutory categories of handicap. Whilst recognising that about 20 per cent of children experienced learning difficulties at some time during their education, Warnock suggested that the 2 per cent of children with the most significant difficulties should be assessed by a multi-disciplinary team and their SEN recorded formally, along with a legally binding statement by the authority of how it intended to address these needs. These recommendations were incorporated into the Education (Scotland) Act 1980. The formal document was called the record of needs in Scotland and its English equivalent was termed the statement of needs.

The report published by Her Majesty's Inspectorate (HMI) in Scotland entitled *The Education of Pupils with Learning Difficulties in Primary and Secondary Schools* (SED, 1978) questioned the received wisdom concerning the nature and origins of learning difficulties and what schools should do to help children who were experiencing such problems. HMI were highly critical of the permanent segregation of lower achieving children within mainstream schools. Such children should be educated alongside their peers but rather than expecting the child to accommodate to a curriculum which might be too difficult or to teaching methods geared to the average child, the onus should be on the mainstream teacher, assisted by the newly-styled learning support teacher, to accommodate the needs of each child. This should be done through the use of differentiated teaching materials and appropriate pedagogy. Looking at the proposals in some detail, it was argued that the focus of remedial education on 'basic skills and numeracy' was too limited. The concept should be broadened to include 'a wider and more diverse range of pupils including those who have trouble coping with these ideas and concepts . . . [and those] whose problems are the result of discontinuity . . . [i.e.] frequent absence or change of school' (para 4.2). HMI were also critical of the diagnostic techniques used (paras 4.4 and 4.5). Identification and assessment of learning difficulties was seen as too dependent on standardised tests of basic reading and number, as establishing 'the point of onset of difficulty' or uncovering 'deeper problems' (not necessarily educational) which could be the cause of poor performance on basic skills tests, leading to 'adverse effects on [pupils'] whole attitude to school'. The curriculum offered to pupils with learning difficulties was regarded as fundamentally flawed by HMI and new goals were delineated (paras 4.6 to 4.9). These included the following:

- curriculum aims should be the same for all pupils;
- pupils should not all have to study the same things, at the same pace, in the same way;
- objectives for pupils should take into account their age, aptitude and ability;
- the curriculum must sustain skill and interest and get pupils across the 'plateau of learning';
- demands on pupils for higher skill and interest must be not only appropriate but also sufficiently challenging;
- de-contextualised activity, such as routine drilling, should be avoided;
- reducing or dropping aspects of the curriculum for individual pupils who require greater provision for the development of basic skills should not be at the expense of enjoyable or creative activities, or those which offer experience of success. (Allan *et al.*, 1991)

In relation to pedagogy (para 4.10), an increase in 'discussion' and a combination of class, group and individual methods for both secondary and primary schools were called for. Rather than undertaking separate work with children experiencing difficulty in learning, the emphasis should be on the preparation of differentiated learning materials. In general, HMI recommended less use of whole class teaching and more use of group and individual work. This is in interesting contrast with recent pronouncements by the Scotttish HMI (SOEID, 1996a) which, in the light of Scotland's relatively poor showing in international league tables, suggest that there should be a return to more direct teaching, possibly in the form of whole class teaching. These more recent shifts in policy are discussed in more detail in a later section.

The key to rethinking provision for children with learning difficulties, HMI decided, was to refashion the role of the learning support teacher and that teacher's relationship to the mainstream teacher. The following four main roles for the former were indicated:

- acting as a consultant to staff and members of the school management team;
- in co-operation with class and subject teachers offering tutorial support and supportive help in their normal classes to pupils with learning difficulties in any areas of the curriculum;
- providing personal tuition and support for pupils with severe learning difficulties in the process of communication and computation; and
- providing, arranging for or contributing to special services within the school.

A firm message to mainstream teachers, however, was that children with learning difficulties should not be seen as the sole responsibility of the learning support teacher, but primarily of the mainstream class teacher who would draw on the support teacher's knowledge and expertise without passing over ultimate responsibility. Despite this shared responsibility, the role of the learning support teacher was couched in extremely wide terms. Elaborating on the four main roles identified above, HMI indicated that the learning support teacher should carry out a number of other tasks including initiating and contributing to staff development; offering a haven for pupils with 'temporary emotional upsets' and for pupils being phased back into mainstream school after a period in residential or special schools; offering a facility in the school whereby pupils can be observed and assessed for a short but intensive period; and offering special expertise in the use of micro-technology, information technology, particularly in relation to differentiation of the curriculum and the analysis and adaptation of published schemes.

From their lowly origins as teachers of backward pupils, it appeared that learning support teachers were being urged to adopt one of the most challenging roles in the school. Recognising opportunities for the expansion of this market, colleges of education in Scotland (now incorporated into universities) upgraded their in-service training programmes, offering courses at certificate, diploma and masters levels. Nonetheless, many teachers who adopted the mantle of learning support expert in school continued to lack a specialist qualification and questions remained as to whether they possessed the necessary power and authority to bring about radical change in school. Recently, the role of the learning support teacher has expanded even further, as many assume responsibility for the management of IEPs (see Chapter 5) and of a growing number of classroom assistants.

Conclusion

This chapter traced the early development of provision for children with SEN in Scotland. Always lagging behind developments in mainstream schooling, education for children with SEN was relatively late to develop. Provision for children with sensory impairments developed most rapidly, with schooling for children with complex difficulties lagging far behind. It was not until the mid-1970s that responsibility for the latter group was transferred to education from health. Additional resources were often allocated to children with SEN in the form of smaller class sizes. On the other hand, stigma also accompanied the diagnosis of a need for 'special educational treatment'. The development of schooling for this group of children was informed by both philanthropic concerns, seeing education as a social good in itself, and human capital considerations, suggesting that training for low-level employment was preferable to the expectation of a life of idleness. The reports of the Warnock Committee and the Scottish HMI were ground-breaking in shifting the emphasis from identifying the child's difficulties to focusing on how the school environment could be modified to allow much higher levels of inclusion. These themes are developed further in subsequent chapters.

Chapter 2

JUSTICE IN SPECIAL EDUCATIONAL
NEEDS ASSESSMENTS:
SOME SCOTTISH/ENGLISH COMPARISONS

Introduction

The Education (Scotland) Act 1980 (as amended), which implemented many of the Warnock Committee's recommendations, was a product of the social democratic political agenda of the 1970s. It was implemented, however, in the very different political climate of the 1980s and 1990s, where the major concern was to increase efficiency and effectiveness by introducing the disciplines of the market into the public sector. In this chapter, the development of special needs provision in the 1990s is described, and is contrasted with developments over the same period in England. The chapter begins with a discussion of competing social policy frameworks and the type of procedural justice which they afford. Drawing on a number of earlier studies (Kirp, 1982; Mashaw,1983; Adler and Sainsbury, 1991; Adler, 2001) and findings from a recent ESRC funded research project (Riddell *et al.*, 2000; 2002; 2005), recent SEN policy in Scotland and England is compared. By making comparisons across different jurisdictions within the UK, policy nuances may be thrown into high relief (Adler, 1997). Debates about the extent of policy convergence or divergence have intensified since the establishment of the Scottish Parliament in 1999 (Mooney and Scott, 2006).

A note on research methods

During the course of the ESRC funded project *Justice Inherent in the Assessment of Special Educational Needs in Scotland and England*, conducted between 1997 and 2000, official policy texts were analysed, interviews conducted with eighteen key informants and questionnaires administered to all local authorities in Scotland and England. On the basis of our preliminary analysis, we chose four case study authorities, two in Scotland and two in England. These differed in relation to their use of mainstream schools to educate children with SEN and also in relation to their rate of appeals. Fifty-nine case studies were conducted with families involved in the process of opening a record or statement of needs. In selecting case studies, efforts were made to include children with a range of difficulties and to maintain a balance between 'contested' and 'non-contested' cases. Case studies consisted of interviews with parents, professionals, education officers and, where appropriate, the child. In addition, some meetings between parents and professionals were observed. Data from this project are drawn upon in this chapter and Chapter 3.

Table 1: Six normative models of administrative justice

Model	Mode of Decision-Making	Legitimating Goal	Mode of Accountability	Characteristic Remedy for User
Bureaucracy	Applying rules	Accuracy	Hierarchical	Administrative review
Professionalism	Applying knowledge	Public service	Interpersonal	Second opinion Complaint to a professional body
Legality	Weighing-up arguments	Fairness	Independent	Appeal to a court or tribunal (public law)
Managerialism	Managerial autonomy	Efficiency gains	Performance measures	Management sanctions Complaint to ombudsman
Consumerism	Active participation	Consumer satisfaction	Consumer charters	'Voice' and/or compensation through Charter
Markets	Price mechanism	Private sector – profit Public sector – efficiency	Commercial viability	'Exit' and/or court action (private law)

Special educational needs and competing policy frameworks

The following SEN policy analysis draws on the work of a number of commentators including Kirp (1982) and Mashaw (1983), and reflects Kirp's insight that 'the way in which a policy problem gets defined says a great deal about how it will be resolved'. Kirp envisages policy frameworks as informed by different versions of procedural justice and existing alongside each other in a state of dynamic tension:

They are pursued by different policy actors for different reasons. They have distinctive potentialities and equally distinctive pathologies, and tend to fall in and out of favour with policy-makers over time. Choosing among these policy frameworks affects the policy system and, vitally, the supposed beneficiaries. (Kirp, 1982, p. 138)

As illustrated in Table 1, each policy framework is characterised by specific forms of decision-making, legitimating goal, nature of accountability and characteristic remedy. The first three policy frameworks in Table 1 are those which have dominated the field of SEN until very recently. Bureaucracy uses rules as the basis for decision-making, promises accuracy and consistency, is hierarchical and if there is evidence of malfunction then administrative review is the remedy which is likely to be applied. The professional policy framework operates by applying professional judgement, seeks legitimacy through claiming to place the client's interests above those of the practitioner, accountability is to clients and other professionals and, if there is dissatisfaction, then a client may complain to a professional body. A policy framework based on legal principles weighs up arguments to determine fair outcomes, which offer it legitimacy. It claims to be independent (hence the depiction of Justice as blind) and appeal is to a court or tribunal.

Other frameworks, specifically managerialism, consumerism and markets, became increasingly important during the 1990s, particularly in England (see below for further discussion). Managerialism refers to attempts to regulate public services with a view to increasing efficiency, effectiveness and value for money (Clarke and Newman, 1997; Newman, 2001). To achieve efficiency gains, performance measures are used to assess whether individuals and services have attained pre-specified outcomes. If targets are not met, management sanctions may be applied, which are likely to involve financial penalties or the loss of contracts. Dissatisfied users may complain to the ombudsman. Consumerism, which has flourished since the late 1980s, is based on the view that service users should have a major say in the nature and delivery of public services. Citizenship is seen increasingly in terms of individual members of the public adopting the role of critical consumer, with consumer charters providing information on the nature and quality of services people have a right to expect. Individuals are thus empowered to shape services through exercising 'voice'. Redress is through complaints procedures and compensation may be paid to those with a legitimate grievance with regard to service quality. Finally, markets have played an increasingly important role in the delivery of public services since the 1980s, and are seen as the means of raising standards and achieving better value for money. People are increasingly given the power to choose between existing services, with the expectation that popular services will expand and flourish, whilst unpopular services will wither and die. The role of government is construed as creating the conditions in which competition between different service providers may flourish, occasionally intervening to rectify market failure. The mode of accountability within this version of procedural justice is commercial viability and the characteristic remedy for those dissatisfied with services is to exercise their power of exit by choosing a different service. It is interesting to note that managerialism, consumerism and marketisation were originally promoted by successive Conservative administrations during the 1980s and 1990s, but have since been embraced by the Labour government in Westminster and, to a lesser extent, by the Labour–Liberal coalition administration at Holyrood.

Policy issues are not usually expressed in terms of a single policy framework; indeed they are more commonly described in terms of composite policy frameworks. Interest groups may suggest that their perspective reflects superior values to those of other contenders, but in practice policy frameworks have different strengths and weaknesses and trade-offs are made between them. Thus, for example, the professional policy framework emphasises service and the need to provide individual solutions to particular problems, but provides few opportunities for legal recourse if the service user disagrees with the professional's perception of the problem. A policy framework based on legality promises to judge individual claims for resources fairly, but the negative trade-off might be that parents who are poor and inarticulate may not be in a position to claim their rights. Such a policy framework has no concern for systemic equity and collective justice. A bureaucratic policy framework might score highly on sticking to agreed procedures, but may be inflexible and unable to meet individual needs. Kirp's analysis thus makes clear that establishing the dominance of a policy framework is a highly political activity, since proponents of different frameworks are in competition with each other.

In the following paragraphs, the development of SEN policy frameworks in Scotland and England in the post-Warnock decades is explored, followed in Chapter 3 by an examination of the implementation of national policies at local level.

Special educational needs policy in Scotland since the 1980s

Following the Education (Scotland) Act 1980 (as amended), SEN policy in Scotland developed relatively slowly for two decades, reflecting elements of bureaucracy, professionalism and legality. Under the 1980 Act, education authorities had a duty to secure adequate and efficient provision of school education for their area, including provision for SEN. Education authorities were required to establish which children belonging to their area, who were two years of age or over but under school leaving age, had pronounced, specific or complex SEN which required continuing review. They had a duty to open and keep a record of needs for any child who, following assessment, was found to have such needs. Education authorities were also able, but not obliged, to open a record of needs for children under the age of two. Parents had a duty to ensure that their children of school age received efficient education suitable for their age, aptitude and ability either by sending them to a school under the management of an education authority or by other means.

If parents believed that education authorities were failing in their duty to provide adequate and efficient education, then they had a right of appeal under Section 70 of the Education (Scotland) Act 1980. Dissatisfaction with the process of recording might also result in an appeal to the Secretary of State or, after devolution, Scottish Ministers. The six areas which were open to appeal were the following: the local authority's decision not to open a record or discontinue it after review; the local authority's decision to open a record or continue it after review; the content of Part 3b of the record (summary of the child's impairments); the contents of Part 4 of the record (statement of the child's SEN); the content of Part 6 (school placement); and refusal of a placing request. Appeals in relation to school placement were to the Education Appeal Committee run by the local authority and appeals against this committee's decision were made to the Sheriff Court. Appeals in relation to the record were made to Scottish Ministers. Furthermore, complaints of maladministration could be made to the ombudsman.

Following the 1980 Act, it is evident that within the sphere of SEN policy in Scotland, three particular policy frameworks were in play: bureaucracy, professional and legal. Rules were laid out pertaining to assessment and recording, such as the requirement for multi-professional assessment and statutory letters. A key role was allocated to professionals in deciding which children merited assessment and the type of provision which was likely to meet their needs. Finally, legality was evident in the specification of avenues for appeal. However, when we look more closely at the SEN policy framework in Scotland in the 1980s and 1990s, it is evident that the professional policy framework dominated and below we explore this in more detail.

It is interesting to note that, compared with England, where a *Code of Practice* with quasi-legal status was introduced in 1994 (DfE, 1994a), no such instrument existed in Scotland until the passage of the Education (Additional Support for Learning) (Scotland) Act 2004 (see later discussion). Circular 4/96 (SOEID, 1996a) and the *Manual of Good Practice* (SOEID, 1998a) provided guidance on good practice and were much less prescriptive than the English Code of Practice. Circular 4/96, for example, emphasised the need for flexible approaches to recording, reflecting circumstances in local authorities rather than fixed and consistent national policies. There was no attempt to specify in detail which children should receive a record of needs, and this led to variable local practices (see Chapter 4 which deals with evidence on inclusion). Although statutory assessment procedures were tightly specified (SOEID, 1996a) the school-based stages of assessment were left to the school's discretion. There was no requirement to have a register of all children with SEN and no regulatory provision for review of children who had SEN but were not recorded. Whilst it might have been expected that the relatively loose criteria for opening a record of needs in Scotland would lead to a higher rate of recording in Scotland, in fact the reverse was true (In 2000, about 2 per cent of Scottish school-aged children had a record of needs compared with 3 per cent of English children having a statement of needs). This suggests that Scottish professionals used the fluidity of the system to resist inflationary pressures on recording. English parents, on the other hand, used the emerging consumerist policy framework to push for greater resources channelled towards individual children, reflected in higher rates of statementing.

In addition to recording criteria, in Scotland many procedural matters were relatively loosely defined. For example, Circular 4/96 stipulated that the period between notification by the authority that an assessment might be necessary through to the opening of the record should not exceed 6 months. However, although Circular 4/96 suggested: 'it is good practice and courteous if the reasons for this can be promptly explained to parents', no penalties were incurred by local education authorities where delays occurred. The Accounts Commission for Scotland (Accounts Commission for Scotland, 2002) noted that the average time taken for assessment was 28 weeks. However, this masked wide variation, with six councils taking on average less than 20 weeks. Slightly less than 10 per cent of assessments took more than a year to complete, while three councils reported that more than 25 per cent of their assessments took longer than a year to complete. Compared with data published two years earlier, it appeared that assessments were being completed more rapidly.

In England, as we shall see below, greater efforts have been made to empower parents, leading to a consumerist approach in some local authorities (see Chapter 3). In Scotland, fewer efforts have been made to involve parents. The Scottish Office published the document *A Parents' Guide to Special Educational Needs* in 1993, equivalent to the DfE's parental guide of 1994 (DfE, 1994b). The guide emphasised the importance of flexibility at local levels for professionals to decide on appropriate forms of provision and dealt with appeals in a fairly cursory manner. The fact that, in Scotland, parents had no right of appeal against the provisions stipulated in the record was glossed over and the document failed to mention the possibility of making a complaint of maladministration to the ombudsman. This might explain why no complaint involving the assessment of SEN has ever been the subject of a formal investigation by the ombudsman in Scotland. In contrast, the annual number of reports involving SEN issued by the Commission for Local Administration in England has been between 20 and 55 per annum.

In addition to the lack of specificity of the record compared with the statement of needs, the major difference between Scotland and England in relation to SEN has been the lack of a robust appeals system north of the Border. Parents have been deterred from appealing to Scottish Ministers because the system has been lengthy and secretive. The fact that it was not possible to appeal in relation to the content of the record also made the system less meaningful. The more radical approach of the Special Educational Needs Tribunal (SENT) in England is discussed below.

Since the advent of the Scottish Parliament in 1999, the policy stasis of the 1980s and 1990s has shifted, with much greater discussion and implementation of new policies. For example, the Education (Standards in Scotland's Schools etc.) (Scotland) Act 2000 established a presumption that all children would be educated in mainstream schools. Exceptionally, children might be educated in a special setting if a mainstream placement would not be suitable to a child's ability or aptitude; would not be compatible with the provision of efficient education for other children or would result in unreasonable public expenditure that would not ordinarily occur. In making a decision on placement, the wishes of the child and parents must be taken into account. This legislation, in terms of underscoring the expectation of mainstream placement, is backed up by draft legislation on planning for pupils with SEN. The Education (Disability Strategies and Pupils' Educational Records) (Scotland) Act 2001 placed a duty on educational providers to produce accessibility strategies, indicating their plans to make both the curriculum and the built environment accessible to all children. The Act supported the requirements of the Disability Discrimination Act as amended by the Special Educational Needs and Disability Act 2001, which is discussed more fully in Chapter 6.

There has also been far greater emphasis on the development of systems to encourage joined-up government and social inclusion. The report *For Scotland's Children* (Scottish Executive, 2001b), for example, explores key issues with regard to the integration of children's services in Scotland. A number of important recommendations are made, including the development of shared financial arrangements between health, social work and education, the development of a modular information and assessment framework and the appointment of a Children's Commissioner. In addition, there has been a renewed focus on the experience of disadvantaged and disaffected children and young people. For example, the report *Better Behaviour – Better Learning* (Scottish Executive, 2001a) made a number of important recommendations including the appointment of additional staff to support children's behaviour and learning, and also advocated the merger of behaviour and learning support departments to avoid artificial divisions between children with behavioural difficulties and those with learning difficulties.

The measure which is likely to have the most significant impact on future provision is the Education (Additional Support for Learning) (Scotland) Act 2004, implemented from November 2005. Earlier legislation defined a child as having SEN if they had much greater difficulty in learning than most other children of their own age, or suffered from a disability or handicap preventing them from being educated with their own peer group, or were under five years old and belonged to either of these groups. The law, however, did not cover children or young people who had difficulties arising from other factors, such as being taught in a language they did not speak at home.

The new definition of additional support needs, as specified in Section 1 of the Education (Additional Support for Learning) (Scotland) Act 2004, is much broader:

> A child or young person has additional support needs for the purposes of this Act where, for whatever reason, the child or young person is, or is likely to be, unable without the provision of additional support to benefit from school education provided or to be provided for the child or young person.

Other agencies include any other local education authority, any local authority (e.g. services provided by social work) and any Health Board or NHS Trust. Children requiring additional support to benefit from education may include disabled children, those looked after by the local authority, children from Gipsy and Traveller families, those with English as an additional language, children of refugees and asylum seekers and children from socially disadvantaged backgrounds. Whilst recognising that children may experience multiple layers of disadvantage, it will be important to monitor which children come to be defined as having additional support needs, and whether the definition of additional support needs works equally well for all. The Act abolished the record of needs and established a new document, the Co-ordinated Support Plan (CSP), for recording children's difficulties in learning and specifying the support to be given.

Qualification criteria for a CSP are tightly specified. According to the Code of Practice entitled *Supporting Children's Learning* (Scottish Executive, 2005), a child will qualify for a CSP if he or she has additional support needs arising from one or more complex factors or multiple factors, and if they require additional support to be provided by the education authority and by one or more appropriate agencies. This is quite a restricted definition, and would, for example, exclude a blind child receiving education but no additional services from other agencies. In this particular case, the child might receive an IEP which would specify long- and short-term educational goals. However, unlike the US Individual Education Plan (Florian and Pullin, 2000), Scottish IEPs do not have to specify additional resources, are not legally binding on the school or the local authority and do not have a route to legal redress. They are also unlikely to involve multi-disciplinary teams (see Chapter 5 and Kane *et al.*, 2003).

The new legislation is somewhat vague about the local authorities' duties *vis-à-vis* the assessment of additional support needs and, according to the Code of Practice, 'The Act does not prescribe any particular model of assessment or intervention' (Scottish Executive, 2005, p. 26). Appropriate agencies (e.g. health, social work) have a duty to assist an education authority in assessment, intervention, planning, provision and review, unless this is prejudicial to the agency's other function. Overall, it appears that multi-professional assessments, which were mandatory in the context of opening a record of needs, are less likely to take place under the terms of the new legislation, and drawn-out legal wrangles appear inevitable if another agency declines to provide the support which might be deemed necessary. For most children, assessment is likely to be much less formal and will depend on the discretion of the local authority and the school. In most cases, the responsibility for assessment is likely to lie with the learning support teacher, but in the absence of mandatory specialist qualifications, knowledge of diagnostic assessment is likely to vary greatly between schools.

As noted above, parents of children with SEN in Scotland have traditionally had weaker rights of appeal compared with their counterparts in England and other parts of the UK, and in this regard the establishment of an Additional Support Needs Tribunal is a significant new development. Parents can appeal all aspects of the CSP, including provision, decisions to draw up or not to draw up a CSP, to discontinue or not to review a CSP and delays in drawing up or not drawing up a CSP. However, the qualification criteria for accessing the Additional Support Needs Tribunal are very stringent. Only those who already have a CSP, or who can show that they have a reasonable case for arguing that they meet the criteria for such a plan, are eligibly to make a reference to the Tribunal. This automatically rules out parents whose children have very significant disabilities, but are receiving all their services from education. The Scottish Executive may thus have created a Catch-22 situation: only those who qualify, or believe they qualify, for a CSP may make a reference to the Tribunal, but the qualification criteria for a CSP have been set so high that only a very small proportion (possibly less than 0.5 per cent of all children) are likely to qualify. Unlike England and Wales, where the Special Educational Needs and Disability Tribunal (SENDIST) now hears disability discrimination cases, in Scotland these are still heard by the Sheriff Court. In England, when the Special Educational Needs Tribunal (SENT) was introduced in 1994, cases in the first year were threefold greater than expected. In Scotland at the time of writing (June 2006), even though the Tribunal had been operational for six months, very few references had been made.

Parents whose children have additional support needs but who do not meet the criteria for a CSP may request independent adjudication if there is a dispute with the local authority. Adjudicators are appointed by the Scottish

Executive and make decisions on the basis of written documents submitted by the local authority and the parents. There is no hearing and the process appears to lack transparency and independence. Potentially, however, there could be far more cases requiring adjudication compared with the number which are likely to be heard by the Additional Support Needs Tribunal.

Another important measure in the legislation is the requirement for local authorities to have independent mediation schemes in place to provide advice and support to parents and to help resolve disputes between parents and local authorities. Whilst mediation schemes may empower parents, there is no requirement on local authorities to provide access to advocacy services. As a result, some people may be prevented from using mediation services effectively because of their own disadvantage or disability. The success of mediation schemes, particularly in reaching socially disadvantaged and excluded parents, therefore needs to be monitored.

To summarise, whilst policy frameworks rooted in bureaucracy, profession and legal system were all evident in Scottish SEN policy in the 1980s and 1990s, professionalism was the dominant framework. Positive trade-offs included an emphasis on meeting the needs of the child and the family in a flexible way. Negative trade-offs were a lack of concern for parents' and children's rights and a lack of consistency in policy implementation. The recent consultation paper on assessment and recording and the government's response indicates a move towards legality and consumerism, with local authorities having a duty to provide parents with better information and allowing them enhanced rights of appeal.

Special educational needs policy and change in England

SEN policy in England in the 1980s, as in Scotland, reflected a balance between the traditional forms of procedural justice based on bureaucracy, professionalism and the legal system. Under the terms of the 1993 Education Act, a number of significant changes took place, increasingly reflecting the wider agenda of marketisation, managerialism and consumerism within the public sector. Parents' organisations in England, arguably stronger than their Scottish counterparts, played an active role in driving reforms. It was believed that some local authorities were failing to put enough funding into the education of children with SEN, and as a result voluntary organisations, including the Council for Disabled Children, campaigned for a tighter legal framework. The 1993 Education Act in England required the Secretary of State to publish a Code of Practice to regulate the assessment and statementing of children with SEN. From September 1994, all state schools were obliged to have regard to the *Code of Practice on the Identification and Assessment of Special Educational Needs* (DfE, 1994b) and publish information about their policies for children with SEN. Each school's governing body had to include a named individual with particular responsibility for SEN provision.

The Code of Practice's requirements necessitated the identification of a Special Educational Needs Co-ordinator (SENCO) or co-ordinating team in each school and in many schools a new appointment had to be made. The role of the SENCO was to implement the school-based stages of assessment and to co-ordinate reviews for all children with SEN. The Code laid down very strict time lines for the completion of the various stages of assessment and statementing, the entire process taking less than seven months, with a particularly tight two-week period allowed for the drafting of the statement. Illness of local education authority staff was not regarded as sufficient excuse for non-completion, although illness or bereavement of the family would count as a good reason for delay. The Commission for Local Administration in England published data on average assessment times in each local authority, and failure to comply with these timescales might justify a complaint of maladministration being lodged with the ombudsman (DfE, 1994b).

In addition to describing how assessment and statementing should be conducted, the Code also specified criteria for triggering assessment and opening a statement in relation to the following categories: learning difficulties, specific learning difficulties (for example, dyslexia), emotional and behavioural difficulties, physical disabilities, hearing impairments, visual impairments, speech and language difficulties, and medical conditions. This might be interpreted as a move away from the anti-labelling approach advocated by Warnock in favour of a recognition of types of impairment and attendant educational difficulties.

The 1993 Education Act also established a parent's right to take a case to a SENT, set up in 1994 and hearing its first cases in 1995. The aim of the SENT was to act as final arbiter where consensus had broken down between parent and the local education authority. Each year since its inception, there has been an increase in the number of appeals referred to the Tribunal and these were unevenly distributed throughout the country. London boroughs had the highest rates of appeal, at around 4.5 per 10,000 pupils (Special Educational Needs Tribunal, 2000). There were also relatively high rates of appeal in the south-east and pockets in the north-west.

Parents were able to appeal to the SENT with regard to the nominated school or the level of resources specified on the statement of needs. Legal representation was used by about 11 per cent of parents and 14 per cent of parents made use of lay representation, often provided by the Independent Panel for Special Educational Advice (IPSEA) or a voluntary organisation such as the British Dyslexia Association. Legal aid was not available to individuals bringing cases to the SENT. About a third of parents presented independent assessments as evidence to the Tribunal and these appeared to influence the outcome of the appeal in favour of the parent (Harris, 1997). The advent of the SENT was indicative of the growing importance of the legal and consumerist policy frameworks in England, with individual parents empowered to seek justice from an impartial body. Since 2002, the Tribunal in England, which has been renamed the Special Educational Needs and Disability Tribunal (SENDIST), also hears cases of disability discrimination.

Recognising the danger that a rapid swing towards a legal policy framework might lead to escalating and unmanageable costs, the Department for Education and Employment (DfEE) included an element within the Grants for Education, Support and Training (GEST) programme, initially for three years and subsequently extended, to fund the development of Parent Partnership Schemes. The main objectives of the programme were to encourage active partnership between parents and professionals with a view to minimising conflict and reducing the number of statutory SEN appeals (Wolfendale and Cook, 1997). The Department for Education and Skills (DfES) has also signalled its intention to reduce reliance on statements (Pinney, 2004; Audit Commission, 2002), but a much stronger voluntary sector lobby in England has so far warded off attempts to abolish the statement of needs.

To summarise, in England during the 1990s the traditional frameworks of bureaucracy, professionalism and legality persisted. However, there was a grater emphasis on legality through the establishment of the SENT. New frameworks were also introduced. Managerialism was evident in the regulation of the performance of schools and local authorities through the Code of Practice. Performance indicators were used to specify and monitor desirable outcomes. Consumerism was also increasingly in evidence, with parents being actively encouraged to take a more active role in the process of assessment and statementing, and to appeal if dissatisfied. Local authorities were obliged to make parents aware of the choice of school and other types of provision available to them, encouraging the operation of a market in the field of SEN with parents, at least in theory, having more opportunity for choice and control over services.

It is important to recognise that particular policy frameworks have both positive and negative trade-offs. The greater emphasis on consumerism, legality and markets meant that parents were able to exert more control over the services on offer. However, this produced a number of pressures within the system. The Green Paper *Excellence for All Children: Meeting Special Educational Needs* (DfEE, 1997) drew attention to the rapid acceleration in the number of children with statements in mainstream primary and secondary schools and the pressure on resources which this produced. It was suggested that the number of statements should be reduced and ultimately the system should be scrapped, although this produced an outcry from parents' groups and voluntary organisations and was therefore not pursued.

The operation of the Code of Practice in schools has also involved both positive and negative trade-offs. There is evidence that SENCOs have experienced a significant increase in their administrative responsibilities, spend less time with children and are suffering considerable stress (Male and May, 1997). However, their status has risen markedly in the eyes of their colleagues as a result of their new place in the school bureaucracy and their close links with the senior management team and the local education authority (Garner, 1996). Senior figures in local education authorities have a generally positive view of the Code because of its administrative clarity and its ready fit with bureaucracy and managerialism (Millward and Skidmore, 1998). The negative trade-off, according to Vincent *et al.* (1996), is the growing curtailment of the professional discretion traditionally enjoyed by teachers, educational psychologists and junior local education authority officers.

The impact of the SENT (now SENDIST) in promoting legality and consumerism has also both positive and negative aspects (Harris, 1997; Evans, 1998; 1999). On the positive side, it is seen as non-intimidating, user-friendly and impartial. On the negative side, it was seen as 'a weapon of the middle classes' (Education Officer cited by Evans, 1998) thus undermining the local education authorities' attempts to ensure equity of resource allocation. There are concerns that some parents are much more able than others to adopt the role of the critical consumer, with few appeals being made from people living in socially disadvantaged areas and from minority ethnic families. The promotion by local education authorities of Parent Partnership Schemes might be seen as a deliberate attempt to tilt the balance away from legality and consumerism and towards professionalism. The Special Educational Needs and Disability Act 2001 placed a duty on local authorities to provide mediation services to all parents who disagreed with the SEN provision made by the school and/or the local authority regardless of whether the child had a statement of needs. This reflects a wider concern to resolve disputes at source rather than in tribunals, reflecting principles of proportionate dispute resolution (Department of Constitutional Affairs, 2004). Whilst some welcome the focus on more informal routes to justice, others see such developments as possibly compromising an individual's right to access a fair legal process.

There have been recent signs of some changes of direction in England. The revised Code of Practice (DfES, 2001) cut down on regulation, reducing the process of assessment to only two stages. In addition, it required authorities to 'set out' rather than 'specify' the provision to be made to meet children's SEN. Resources to purchase additional classroom assistants were given directly to schools, with no guarantee that they would be used for this purpose. The strategy for SEN (DfES, 2004) underlines the government's commitment to inclusion in the context of the inter-agency strategy set out in the Green Paper *Every Child Matters* (DfES, 2003), but recognises the need for much greater consistency in the quality of inclusive practices. The number of appeals to the SENT continued to rise, and in 1999/2000 2,463 were registered, an increase of just over 2 per cent on the previous year (Annual Report, 1999–2000, Special Educational Needs Tribunal, 2000). More recent statistics from the SENDIST (Special Educational Needs and Disability Tribunal, 2005) show that the Tribunal received 3,215 appeals in 2004–5, slightly fewer than the previous year, although this is probably accounted for by the inception of the Special Educational Needs and Disability Tribunal for Wales, which heard 117 cases which would previously have been dealt with by the SENDIST. A relatively small number of these cases related to disability discrimination, and the influx of such cases which had been anticipated had failed to materialise.

Conclusion

Having summarised key policy documents of the 1990s and reviewed evidence of their impact, it is appropriate to consider how SEN policy in England and Scotland may be understood in terms of the policy frameworks outlined earlier. In Scotland in the 1990s, the professional policy framework, backed up by bureaucracy and, to a lesser extent, legality, continued to hold sway and the language of official documents warned parents that although they might act as partners, final decisions on service provision still lay with professionals. The system was relatively unregulated, with no management sanction for time delays in conducting assessments. Educational psychologists retained considerable freedom in deciding which individuals and groups of children were to receive records. Schools did not automatically register all children with SEN and school-based stages of assessment, whilst recommended, were not uniformly applied. Appeals mechanisms were time-consuming, complicated and lacked independence.

In England, a wider repertoire of policy frameworks appears to have been in play, with elements of bureaucracy, professionalism, legality, managerialism, consumerism and marketisation all in evidence. The tighter regulation of assessment and statementing was promoted by voluntary organisations and welcomed by civil servants and senior administrators who saw them as a way of managing the system more effectively and curbing the discretion of less senior officers, educational psychologists and teachers. According to Harris (1997), lawyers also welcomed the changes, recognising education as a fruitful field for future work. Hostility towards tighter regulation was expressed most strongly by 'street level bureaucrats' (Weatherley and Lipsky, 1977; Lipsky, 1980; Vincent *et al.*, 1996) such as SENCOs, educational psychologists and education officers, who have responsibility for implementation but little control over the conditions within which this takes place. Moves towards a wider policy repertoire also produced both positive and negative trade-offs for parents. Bowers and Wilkinson (1998) noted that some parents disliked being part of a tightly rule-bound system, where they were required to respond to communications from the local education authority within strictly specified periods. Some parents were also opposed to the compulsory registration of children with SEN and their regular review, which might be seen as a disciplinary rather than benign mechanism. On the positive side, many parents and voluntary organisations welcomed a more tightly controlled system allowing a greater degree of parental choice and with an inbuilt system of legal redress. A negative trade-off of policy frameworks built on consumerism, legality and the market was the lack of equal access to procedural justice, since there is considerable evidence that socially advantaged parents are in a much better position to act as critical consumers.

In both Scotland and England, the winds of change have been blowing and at the time of writing it is possible to recognise aspects of both convergence and divergence. In Scotland, the additional support for learning legislation is arguably attempting to replace the former dominance of professionalism with a more eclectic policy mix. In England, the revised Code of Practice indicates a desire to return a greater degree of power to professionals, particularly those working in schools, to decide on the distribution of resources to children with SEN. Again, the outcome of this new policy direction is unknown and is certain to be challenged by those seeking to protect the rights of parents and children. A further important unifying measure is the extension of the Disability Discrimination Act 1995 to education, implemented in 2002. This new legislation covers Scotland, England and Wales and indicates a shift away from the professional assessment of needs as the basis for resource distribution. In the future, resource distribution will be based on what is required to allow disabled children and young people to exercise their right to full social inclusion. The implications of the legislation are discussed further in Chapter 6.

Chapter 3

SPECIAL EDUCATIONAL NEEDS
AND JUSTICE IN PRACTICE:
SOME LOCAL AUTHORITY CASE STUDIES

Introduction

In Chapter 2, the policy frameworks underpinning post-war SEN policy were described. It was noted that until relatively recently, the dominant frameworks were based on professionalism, bureaucracy and legality. In England during the 1980s and 1990s, there was a growth in the influence of different policy frameworks based on managerialism, consumerism and markets. Whilst these elements were also present in Scotland, professionalism remained the dominant influence. Systems in both England and Scotland are undergoing change at the moment, with a growing emphasis in both countries on mixed economies of welfare. The White Paper *Modernising Government* (Cabinet Office, 1999) stated a commitment to the development of public services which were of high quality and efficient, 'joined up' and strategic and focused on public service users, not the interests of providers. The documents envisaged a mixed economy of service delivery, with an emphasis on service outcomes. These goals are obviously in line with the further development of managerialism, markets and consumerism across the public sector.

So far the discussion has focused on the broad thrust of public policy at national level. However, in translating policies from the statute book to the local level, there are many opportunities for subversion and transformation as local actors interpret and recreate these policies. This chapter describes the implementation of national policies in four local authorities, two in Scotland and two in England. Like Chapter 2, it draws on research carried out as part of an ESRC project (Riddell *et al.*, 2002) between 1997 and 2000. Having identified some broad differences between Scottish and English policies, our aim was to explore the extent to which these global differences could still be discerned at local level. The four local authorities are explored in relation to the six policy frameworks set out in Table 1. Following the interviews with key informants and the local authority questionnaire survey, case study authorities were selected which appeared to exemplify a particular policy framework. However, in-depth discussion with local policy-makers and parents indicated a more complex picture than had been anticipated. Below, each local authority, and its position within our policy typology, is described. It is important to note that since this research was carried out, procedures for identifying and meeting SEN (now additional support needs) in Scotland have changed, whilst the broad framework in England has remained broadly the same. This research therefore might be seen as a touchstone against which the impact of the new policy framework in Scotland may be considered.

Scottish Local Authority 1: bureaucratised professionalism

Local Authority 1 is a Scottish city which has experienced a long period of industrial decline. Forty-two per cent of the city's population live in an area of deprivation. In 54 per cent of city schools, more than half the children are entitled to free school meals and the city has high rates of unemployment and economic inactivity. More than forty per cent of children in the city are in families dependent on income support. The city has a high and increasing number of single parent households and a relatively high minority ethnic population.

At the time of the research, there were a number of government schemes and plans geared towards addressing problems of poverty and social exclusion. These included a number of Social Inclusion Partnerships, a Healthy Cities Development Plan and a Health Improvement Plan. Due to a major building programme in the 1950s and 1960s, the authority had a great deal of special school provision (31 special schools and three special units attached to mainstream) and as a result 82 per cent of children with records of needs were in special schools. Despite the fact that it did not record children with social, emotional and behavioural difficulties, the authority had a relatively high proportion of recorded children, reflecting high levels of social deprivation in the area. The key policy features of Local Authority 1 are summarised in Table 2.

Practice in this authority was not always in line with the Scottish Executive's advice on parental involvement. For instance, it was recommended that parents should be invited to attend all statutory assessments, but case study parents were only routinely invited to attend the medical assessment. Assessment reports were distributed when requested, but parents had not always seen these prior to case conferences, which made it difficult for them to question professional judgements. At the start of the statutory assessment, parents were given some written information on procedures, but this tended to downplay the legal significance of the record and parents' right of appeal. The Named Person was described as 'someone to whom you can talk and can help you' instead of a technical adviser and advocate. Only one parent among our case studies within this authority used a Named Person as

Table 2: Model Features of Scottish Local Authority 1

Models	Features	Comments
BUREAUCRACY	Local authority stipulates particular phases to be used in record of needs (RoN). Senior officer edits final version of the RoN. Educational psychologists object to being co-opted into the bureaucracy.	Educational psychologist in sole charge of recording process until local authority sends copies of documents to parents and other professionals.
PROFESSIONALISM	Educational psychologists believed to have most influence – considerable power with regard to orchestrating recording process and outcome.	Educational psychologists have vital gate-keeping role in terms of initiating procedures. Believe they are best qualified to guide process.
LEGALITY	Parents sometimes object to school nominated by local authority, but little understanding of process or their role within it.	Parents unaware of potential of recording process to challenge local authority. Routinely given brief written description of process. Procedures within Local Authority Appeals Committee appear to be flawed – lack independence and transparency. No information available on route to redress.
MANAGERIALISM	Accounts Commission for Scotland publishes metrics on time taken to open record of needs, but no other information published.	Local authority takes much longer to open record than recommended 6 month period.
CONSUMERISM	Little local support available to parents. Number of voluntary organisations offer advice to parents on SEN procedures and rights.	Few opportunities for parents to exercise 'voice'. Access to information very limited. Named Person little used – often presented as family friend to act as supporter in meetings, rather than informed advocate.
MARKETS	Information not routinely provided on range of school choices.	Parents sometimes challenge local authority nomination – but do not actively 'play' the educational market.

an advocate. The statutory letters issued within this local authority tended to be legalistic in tone, and the recommended timescale for the opening of a record was not mentioned.

In this authority, the high level of expenditure on SEN was of major concern. Educational psychologists were instructed to write the record in general terms without committing the authority to any specific expenditure. As a result of these pressures, educational psychologists in the authority found themselves pulled in different directions by the conflicting expectations that they could both act as honest brokers giving parents the best possible advice about their children's needs, but also as agents of the local authority, chairing statutory meetings and drafting the record in terms of the resources available to the authority. One educational psychologist suggested that the record of needs was not a productive document because of its generality and another spoke of 'the raging ambiguity of our position' because of the requirement to act as an agent of the authority, whilst simultaneously serving the child's best interests.

Parents were somewhat confused about the purpose of the record and their role within the process. One parent explained that she became so disillusioned with the record of needs that she did not bother to read the final document. Views like this were typically seen by educational psychologists as evidence that the process was too bureaucratic and difficult for parents to understand.

To summarise, the policy framework operating in Local Authority 1 may be characterised as an example of bureaucratised professionalism. Whilst it was claimed that professionals operated independently of the authority, in reality it appeared that they allied themselves with its interests. Opportunities for parents to act as critical consumers, to choose a school or use their legal rights were limited. Other professionals, such as medical officers, who might raise parental expectations by suggesting alternative views of the child's needs, had only marginal involvement.

Scottish Local Authority 2: centralised bureaucracy

Local Authority 2 is a medium-sized predominantly rural Scottish authority. The area has little industry and farming employs increasingly fewer people; tourism is a much bigger employer. There is some rural poverty, with about 12 per cent of children entitled to free school meals. Because of its rural nature, it was never practical to build special schools (the area had only two) because this would have involved children travelling long distances. Instead, special units attached to mainstream schools, some with specific specialisms, had developed. Sixty-nine per cent of recorded children were counted as being in mainstream, although some spent very little or no time in mainstream classes. About 2 per cent of children had records of needs, slightly above the national average.

Scottish Local Authority 2 had developed a centralised bureaucratic system for the management of SEN as presented in Table 3. Some years ago, it was decided that educational psychologists were too closely involved in co-ordinating recording procedures, and this might compromise their position as independent professionals acting on behalf of their client. It

Table 3: Model Features of Scottish Local Authority 2

Models	Features	Comments
BUREAUCRACY	Head of Psychological and Learning Support Services decides if statutory assessment should commence. Area Managers of Learning Support collate assessments. Head of Psychological and Learning Support Services decides if record should be opened. Educational psychologists acknowledge conflict between their professional role and role of local authority.	Educational Psychologists initiate recording process by making recommendation to Head of Psychological and Learning Support Services. Area Managers of Learning Support make final decision. Criteria not agreed by panel as in English local authorities.
PROFESSIONALISM	Educational psychologists recommend to Head of Psychological and Learning Support Services which children should have statutory assessment. Educational psychologists perceive themselves as advocates for parents. Area Managers of Learning Support has responsibility for SEN procedures and managing SEN budget. Parents, schools and other professionals can initiate statutory assessments, but this rarely happens.	Educational psychologists hold gate-keeping role with regard to commencing statutory assessment. Head of Psychological and Learning Support Services personally views and approves all applications.
LEGALITY	Parents viewed by educational psychologists and officers as important in that they could object to school placement named on the record. When dissatisfied, parents quick to challenge terms of record. Authority has relatively high rate of appeals to Scottish Ministers. No complaints to ombudsman.	Parents aware of the potential of the record to challenge the local authority. Information about process restricted to brief by educational psychologist and accompanying literature. Named Person little used. Educational psychologists often alluded to themselves as advocates for parents.
MANAGERIALISM	Data published on time taken to open record.	Time taken to open record much longer than average.
CONSUMERISM	Some local voluntary organisations encourage parents to engage in dialogue with the authority.	Local authority makes little attempt to engage parents in process.
MARKETS	Parents not given list of possible schools. Choice restricted by geography – rural area.	Choice outwith designated special unit discouraged. Only one special school.

was therefore decided to focus the role of the educational psychologist on assessing children's needs and offering advice to schools. The task of orchestrating the recording process was delegated to three area managers, each liaising with a Principal Educational Psychologist and reporting to the Head of Psychological and Learning Support Services (HPLSS). In order to achieve fairness and consistency, the HPLSS makes the final decision in all cases on the opening of a record of needs and resource allocation. Before the opening of a record, schools were required to demonstrate that they had implemented the recommended staged process of intervention. The very centralised decision-making process had a marked impact on the role of educational psychologists and the opportunities for parental involvement which are discussed below.

According to the HPLSS, the record of needs was a document which had outlived its usefulness. He drew attention to the fact that Circular 4/96 states that the record of needs does not need to quantify provision, and this should be specified in the IEP. Research on IEPs (Banks *et al.*, 2001), however, found no examples of provision being specified in these documents. It was argued that learning support needs in particular schools should be established through an annual audit in which schools report children's additional needs to the authority. Overall, it was believed that the record of needs was redundant and simply encouraged some parents to believe that they could extract additional resources from the authority. When parents requested a statutory assessment, they were often told that this was not necessary because provision was already being made for their child as a result of an annual audit of resource needs. This contrasted with the situation in England, where the Code of Practice required the statement of needs to specify all the special educational provision that the local education authority considered appropriate for *all* the child's learning difficulties. The statement was also expected to specify the child's non-educational needs and describe the provision to be made by health and other services. Parents were becoming increasingly restive in Scottish Local Authority 2 and the authority had a significant number of appeals to Scottish Ministers. Because it is not possible to appeal against Part V of the record (the measures proposed by the local authority) parents appealed against the description of the child's SEN and the authority's decision on whether to open a record.

When multi-disciplinary meetings were abolished in Scottish Local Authority 2 in the mid-1990s, educational psychologists first felt bereft of an important role. Subsequently, they recognised that this enabled them to play a more proactive part in advocating for the parents or children, a role which would have been compromised if acting primarily for the authority with the SEN budget in mind. Nonetheless, some educational psychologists still felt that they had been somewhat marginalised and would have preferred greater involvement, although others believed that they were better able to preserve their professional integrity if they remained at arm's length from the process. Schools also felt that they had been squeezed out of the process and the professional perspectives of head teachers, learning support staff and classroom teachers were no longer required. In response to feelings of both the educational psychologists and parents that they had been marginalised and bureaucratic power had become concentrated at a single point in the system, the HPLSS had recently reinstated the formal meeting to discuss the terms of the record of needs, although he still considered that this was not the best use of the authority's resources.

To summarise, Scottish Local Authority 2 exemplified a bureaucratic and highly centralised approach, which marginalised the power and input of professionals and managers. This allowed the HPLSS, originally an educational psychologist, to keep a tight handle on issues of budgetary allocation and to oversee the system for consistency. His view of fairness, however, was not audited by any other interest group, and therefore was likely to be somewhat partial. The type of accountability mechanisms rooted in the Code of Practice were absent in both Scottish local authorities. The only public performance indicator was the measure of time taken to open a record of needs published by the Accounts Commission for Scotland, and both the case study local authorities performed poorly against this indicator. There were also strong similarities between the Scottish case study local authorities in that both were based on a bureaucratic approach and attempted to minimise consumerism and rights approaches. They were also hostile to mangerialism, because of its threats to their autonomy. Professionals were allowed to exercise some degree of discretion, as long as this did not interfere with the smooth running of the bureaucratic system.

English Local Authority 3: benign bureaucracy

English Local Authority 3 is a small metropolitan authority in the heart of an old northern coal field in England serving a relatively homogeneous and largely disadvantaged community. There are few people from minority ethnic backgrounds and a low proportion of people moving into or out of the area. Unemployment in the area is almost double the English national average and a high proportion of people are economically inactive. There is a culture of low educational achievement and aspiration, and the proportion of graduates among the population is half the English average. An Office for Standards in Education (OFSTED) report noted that standards in schools were low compared with national averages and those of similar local authorities. The authority was criticised for 'having done little to raise the profile of education and levels of pupils' achievements' and was seen as having 'complicated and inefficient internal management arrangements'. Criticisms were also made of the local authority's SEN management arrangements, particularly with regard to the time taken to draw up a statement.

In recognition of its high level of social disadvantage and low educational attainments, a number of social inclusion and educational improvement projects were under way. The local authority had Education and Health Action Zones, an Educational Partnership Plan and a School Development and Effectiveness Strategy. Most children were educated in mainstream and the authority had only three special schools, four units attached to mainstream and one stand-alone unit. Slightly less than 2 per cent of the population had statements and 83 per cent of children with statements were educated in mainstream schools. This high use of mainstream schools was not as a result of a major policy change, but rather because special schools had never been built in this area. Some mainstream schools had been adapted to accommodate pupils with physical disabilities while the units offered specialised teaching to children with hearing impairments, specific learning difficulties, autism and behaviour problems. English Local Authority 3 had very low rates of appeals to the SENT and there were also few complaints of maladministration to the Commission for Local Administration.

Table 4 summarises some key features of the authority in terms of the policy frameworks described in Table 1. As noted earlier, the national SEN policy and legal framework in England allows parents greater opportunities to operate as service consumers within a marketised system, whilst at the same time tightening the management regime within which professionals operate. Nonetheless, there were elements of all six models in the authority with evident tensions between them.

Many features of policy and procedure in the local authority were geared towards assisting parents to play an active role in the assessment and statementing of their children and to seek legal redress where appropriate. However, as the low rate of appeal suggests, parents were not closely involved in the process. They did not generally seek to use their power of exit to request a placement in a school other than that suggested by the local authority. In the same way, they did not use their voice as consumers to request different forms of support. For example, most statements simply stated that a child would receive a specific number of hours of additional support from a classroom assistant, and parents did not normally request additional support such as speech therapy. Questions arise as to why the provisions of the 1996 Education Act, which promoted consumerism, markets, and legality, had not had a more radical effect on the nature of parents' participation. It appeared that, although information about their rights was made available, many parents experienced extreme social disadvantage and were therefore not able to make full use of possible choices. For example, with the initial letter, parents were given a DfEE booklet explaining the process of drawing up a statement. However, many parents interviewed did not find this booklet accessible. For a time, a senior officer had hand-delivered all initial notices of the authority's intention to begin the process of statutory assessment.

However, this practice was discontinued because of changes in personnel. It was felt that whilst it had been very worthwhile for some parents in terms of demystifying the process, for others, according to a Senior Officer, it was 'a waste of time because you go and you can tell they're not listening to you'. Instead of providing parents with more help, this officer concluded that there was no point in trying to secure greater involvement because parents lacked understanding and motivation, thus locating the fault with them rather than the system of communication. It was evident from the case studies conducted that parents under social stress were resistant to becoming involved in the statementing process. Others wished for greater involvement but were uncertain about how this might be achieved.

Table 4: Model Features of English Local Authority 3

Models	Features	Comments
BUREAUCRACY	Decision on qualification for statement made by committee made up of professionals and officers working to criteria. Final decision delegated to senior officer.	Most committee members were formerly practising teachers – professionals co-opted into bureaucracy.
PROFESSIONALISM	Educational psychologists seen as being most influential group. Regarded themselves as serving the best interests of the child.	Educational psychologists downplayed their power and influence – did not see themselves acting as gatekeepers to statement of needs.
LEGALITY	Code of Practice sets out clear regulations on parental involvement and Special Educational Needs Tribunal provides accessible route to redress.	Very low rate of appeal to Tribunal or complaint to ombudsman.
MANAGERIALISM	Poor performance in relation to stipulated timescales for opening statement of needs noted – local authority anxious to improve in this regard.	Systems subjected to tighter scrutiny – research seen as contributing to this process.
CONSUMERISM	Firm representation at draft statement stage seen to be effective. Parent Partnership Officer making great efforts to engage with parents.	Parents not well-informed about their rights. Although local authority published information leaflet, not used extensively by parents. Schools sometimes encouraged parents to request greater time allocation for support.
MARKETS	Parents given list of schools from which to choose.	Choice of school restricted to mainstream or unit because of lack of special schools.

It was also evident that the managerialist regime associated with the Code of Practice did not always work to parents' advantage. Professionals almost always met their targets in terms of completing assessments within the prescribed timescale, but sometimes did this by failing to ensure that parents fully understood the procedures. For example, parents were routinely sent copies of all assessment reports with the draft statement as recommended in the Code, but did not receive them at the same time as the professionals and therefore had a shorter period of time to consult and consider the need for further action (for example, requesting a second medical opinion). Nobody went through the reports with parents to make sure they were understood. In addition, parents were given a list of all the possible schools which their child might attend; however, the local authority almost always recommended that the child should be placed in the local mainstream school, thus closing down rather than opening up discussion of alternatives.

On the face of it, parents in English Local Authority 3 were given all the information they needed to use the legal framework, including using their power of exit to select a different type of school from that nominated by the local authority. They were informed of their right of choice and to appeal, and after the delivery of the draft statement were offered two meetings with a senior official in addition to access to a Parent Partnership Officer. If a resolution was not reached after these meetings, parents were encouraged to begin appeals proceedings. Throughout the process, educational psychologists described themselves operating as independent agents. They provided important advice to the local authority officers, but did not make the final decision on whether to open a statement; nor did they draft the statement itself. Despite this independence, a large number of appeals would undoubtedly have added to the educational psychologists' workload and therefore it was not in their interests to encourage parents to appeal. Whereas parents in more socially advantaged areas were able to form their own support groups, draw on the expertise of the voluntary sector and commission independent assessments, these options were less likely to be available in this authority. Parents had access to a Parent Partnership Officer, but their job was understood as reconciling parents to the authority's position, and very few appointed a Named Person to act as an independent advocate. To summarise, whilst the national SEN framework in England emphasised a type of procedural justice based on legality, markets, consumerism and managerialism, elements of post-war bureaucracy and professionalism survived.

English Local Authority 4: consumer-focused managerialism

English Local Authority 4 is an inner London borough with a long-standing Conservative administration. The borough contains some very affluent areas but overall is significantly more disadvantaged than most areas in England. The proportion of pupils eligible for free school meals is well above the national average. The percentage of children with a statement of needs was, at the time of the research, below the national average. The local authority had a high minority ethnic population (53 per cent) and many pupils had English as a second language. Attainment on entry to school and later was generally high for London. One of the council's key priorities was to keep the council tax as low as possible. Local Authority 4's secondary pupils were the lowest funded and its primary pupils the second lowest funded of any inner London borough. There was a strong emphasis on management in the borough and an OFSTED report published in 2000 commended the authority on developing the capacity of its head teachers and senior managers to improve their schools through effective use of management information.

The borough defined its own education objectives in terms of 'challenging schools to raise standards, whilst promoting their autonomy in an education service that encourages diversity and increases parental choice'. To pursue these management goals, the borough had developed systems to track the progress of individual pupils and was therefore able to judge how different schools were performing in value added terms. Rigorous improvement targets were set for schools in relation to management information systems.

The emphasis on parental choice was evident in the pattern of secondary education, where over a third of parents chose out-of-borough or independent schools. Significant numbers of pupils from less affluent neighbouring boroughs moved into the borough's secondary schools. The borough's eighty schools had diverse systems of governance, and included voluntary aided, community and foundation schools as well as schools with Beacon and specialist college status. Choice and diversity were also key themes in the borough's SEN strategy. Following the abolition of the Inner London Education Authority, the borough was left with more than ten special schools. Recently three of these had closed, but a relatively high proportion of children continued to be educated in special schools (57 per cent of all children with statements). The borough had a policy of promoting inclusion and 43 per cent of children with statements attended mainstream schools. There was some concern among the special schools that many were running at under-capacity, leading to increased unit costs.

Parents were well informed of their rights and since 1998 had been assisted by the Parent Partnership Service. Parents' forum meetings were held on a termly basis and annual parents' conferences were well supported. The borough had a relatively high proportion of appeals to the Special Educational Needs Tribunal. In 1999/2000, 16 appeals were heard. Fifty-six appeals were registered between 1997 and 2000, although of these 40 per cent were withdrawn before the hearing took place. The appeals mostly concerned refusal of the local authority to make a statutory assessment or the school named in the statement. In 1999/2000, 70 per cent of cases were won by the local authority. In addition to appeals to the SENT, nine complaints, concerning alleged delay to type of provision, had been made to the Commissioner for Local Administration. The ombudsman had decided either that there was no case to answer or that maladministration had not occurred. Since the local authority had tightened up its procedures, opening virtually all its statements within the prescribed timescale, complaints had become rare.

As summarised in Table 5, English Local Authority 4 exemplified many features of new managerialism, characterised by high levels of delegation from the centre to the schools, but with control from the centre maintained by the strict management of performance.

Within the field of SEN, this was exemplified by the insistence on adherence to strict time limits and procedures for statutory assessment and statementing. Two area-based teams of case managers were responsible for the management of assessment and statementing and their role was clearly separated from that of the educational psychologists, whose remit was to offer professional advice on the difficulties and needs of particular children. All systems were computerised and standard letters were issued automatically once the assessment procedure was initiated. The Senior Officer said that the 18-week deadline in issuing the draft statement and the 26-week deadline for issuing the final statement imposed great pressures on case managers, who were closely scrutinised by senior officers and elected members. These pressures were passed on to professionals and parents themselves. Even if parental agreement had not been secured, the local authority often issued the draft statement, in the knowledge that the SENT would automatically find against them if there was any delay. The tight timescale for the production of the final statement sometimes meant that parents did not have enough time to visit all the schools they were considering.

A decision on issuing a statement was made by a panel with reference to tightly specified criteria, which were used to place each child in a band according to the extent of their additional needs. This was to ensure consistency and fairness in resource allocation and each child's banding was regularly reviewed. The Parent Partnership Co-ordinator commented that in her view the local authority's systems were 'fair and they treat everybody the same'. This helped to overcome social class injustices which might otherwise arise. The application of very strict criteria was not only perceived to be fair, but also served the local education authority's policy objective of reducing the number of children with statements of needs. The down-side of this bureaucratic approach was that, although professionals were involved in the decision-making process, their ability to bend rules in unusual cases was reduced, leading parents to perceive the system as inflexible.

It was evident that Local Authority 4 had undergone a significant cultural change since the 1980s, replacing traditional systems of bureaucracy and

Table 5: Model Features of English Local Authority 4

Models	Features	Comments
BUREAUCRACY	Published criteria used to decide which children qualify for statement of needs. Many decisions taken by officers working alone or as part of small panel. Parents believed there was a lack of flexibility in decision-making on out-of-borough special school placement.	Panel membership split between officer and professionals.
PROFESSIONALISM	Educational psychologists most influential group, acting as gatekeepers to statutory assessment.	Educational psychologists downplayed their influence, believing they were no more powerful than any other professionals.
LEGALITY	Active Parent Partnership Co-ordinator and voluntary organisations produced high levels of awareness of rights and routes of redress. High level of Tribunal appeals suggests active and well-informed parents.	Senior Officer believed there was inevitable tensions between authority's concern with systemic fairness and Tribunal's concern for individual child. Intervention of legal representation sometimes produced maverick judgements. Few Tribunal cases from minority ethnic groups.
MANAGERIALISM	Handbook issues to all staff setting out procedures and timescales. Concern to adhere to specified timelines. Strict criteria used to inform statementing and resourcing policies.	High levels of complaints to ombudsman indicate parents aware of rights in relation to delivery of high quality public services.
CONSUMERISM	High use of Parent Partnership Co-ordinator and Named Persons. Termly parents' forum meetings organised by local authority. Some concerns that the agenda is driven by middle-class parents' preoccupations. Active voluntary organisations, some campaigning for inclusion and some to defend special schools.	Parents not well-informed about their rights. Although local authority published information leaflet, not used extensively by parents. Schools sometimes encouraged parents to request greater time allocation for support. Efforts by Parent Partnership Co-ordinator to extend voice to socially excluded groups. Believed this was local authority's major strength compared with neighbouring authorities.
MARKETS	High level of appeal concerns school nominated by local authority. Some over-subscribed selective schools reluctant to include children with SEN. Particular problems finding placements for children with behavioural difficulties.	Local authority reluctant to agree to placement in independent school or school outwith the authority.

professionalism with a new *modus operandi* based on legality, managerialism, consumerism and markets. Whilst the Senior Officer made it clear that local authority officers were pressurised by these systems, she felt that the use of clear criteria in the system meant that outcomes were fair. She also endorsed the strengthening of parents' rights through the SEN Tribunal, because if the authority had failed to follow proper procedures then the SENT was likely to adjudicate in the parents' favour. The presence of an independent body empowered to make a final decision meant that disputes could be finally resolved. In order to avoid appeals, which staff found very stressful, the local authority had made active efforts to engage parents in the process through the Parent Partnership Service. The Parent Partnership Co-ordinator focused in particular on engaging socially disadvantaged parents who might otherwise be alienated from the process. This helped to counteract the negative trade-off between consumerist, rights and market approaches, which tend to empower those who already enjoy considerable social advantage. The Senior Officer felt, however, that a fundamental tension remained between the Tribunal, which was concerned with individual cases, and the local authority, which was concerned with overall provision. She pointed out that, by taking a case to the SENT, it might be possible for a child with less significant difficulties to obtain disproportionately expensive provision and this raised difficult equal opportunities concerns. In addition, if the outcome depended on the quality of legal representation, then this was likely to produce less favourable outcomes for those who were unrepresented.

The Senior Officer also noted that that highly marketised character of education in English Local Authority 4 had a negative effect on children with SEN, particularly those with behavioural difficulties. Selective schools were heavily over-subscribed and could legitimately refuse a place to a pupil with SEN. Even if a place was available, devolved school management, particularly in relation to admissions and exclusions, meant that the local authority was reluctant to challenge a head teacher's decision to refuse a place. The choices of parents of children with SEN also had a marked effect on the system. Some middle-class parents with dyslexic children requested a place in an independent residential school, which might cost at least £20,000 a year. The local authority often refused such requests because it felt it had adequate provision within the borough. However, such cases were likely to be appealed.

Overall, English Local Authority 4 had strong features of legality, managerialism, consumerism and markets and features of these models tended to reinforce each other. Bureaucracy and professionalism were also evident though muted; whilst educational psychologists played an important role in the process, they were not allowed to orchestrate proceedings or make final decisions on placement. Managerialism had replaced post-war bureaucracy, in that procedures were not simply laid out, but were rigorously enforced and there was a major emphasis on improving performance and delivering services shaped by consumer input.

Conclusion

This chapter has illustrated the tensions between different policy frameworks in local authorities in Scotland and England. Whilst there was evidence of all policy frameworks in each local authority, a different balance appeared to be struck north and south of the Border. In Scotland, professionalism and bureaucracy continued to hold sway, whereas in the English authorities a greater repertoire of policy models was drawn upon. As noted in Chapter 2, each policy framework involves a different set of positive and negative trade-offs. In the two Scottish authorities, the bureaucratic and professional models appeared to offer consistency, a concern with systemic justice and a commitment to serving the best interests of the child. Negative trade-offs included the danger of paternalism, a down-playing of rights and the co-option of professionals into bureaucratic roles which might limit their ability to prioritise their client's interests over those of their employer.

In both English authorities, the influence of a wider range of policy frameworks was evident, with a growing emphasis on legality, managerial-ism, consumerism and markets. Here, too, both positive and negative trade-offs were apparent. Whilst parents enjoyed greater choice, not all were able to fulfil the role of critical consumer. In the London borough, there was a perception that middle-class parents might be able to exert more influence to get the services they wanted and to appeal if dissatisfied. It was certainly the case that very few parents in the northern authority with high levels of social disadvantage were engaged in choosing services, using Parent Partnership Schemes or appealing if dissatisfied. By the same token, the managerialist regime, characterised by the setting of strict targets, placed professionals under pressure and allowed them less time to work creatively with parents.

Overall, it was clear that, whilst national policies were implemented differently in specific local contexts, there was a tendency in Scotland to draw more exclusively on a narrower range of policy frameworks. As noted in Chapter 2, this may change in the future with the reform of the system of recording, which introduces a Code of Practice for the first time, empha-sises the need for mediation and gives some parents access to a tribunal. The extent to which this will challenge the dominance of professionalism and bureaucracy remains to be seen.

Chapter 4

DEFINING AND MEASURING INCLUSION

Introduction

Legislation and official policy documents at national and local level all express a commitment to school inclusion, which is linked to the government's wider social inclusion agenda. The Education (Standards in Scotland's Schools etc.) (Scotland) Act 2000 and the Special Educational Needs and Disability Act 2001 provide the legislative underpinning for inclusion. Beyond legislation, the Scottish Executive has funnelled considerable monies towards local authorities and their schools to promote inclusion. For example funds have been put aside for Alternatives to Exclusion, to raise standards in Scotland's schools (the Excellence Fund), and SEN Innovation Grants. A major educational initiative in 1998 was to pilot New Community Schools, which sought to provide integrated services to children, and was directly linked to the social justice agenda. This programme is now being rolled out across Scotland but with different funding arrangements. The Discipline Task Group in its report *Better Behaviour – Better Learning* (Scottish Executive, 2001a) recommended, amongst other things, that funds be allocated to local authorities to enable the employment of additional staff, such as classroom assistants and home-school link workers, to support positive behaviour. Schools were also encouraged to integrate behaviour and learning support departments to avoid artificial distinctions between children with behavioural or learning difficulties. Finally, the Scottish Executive has indicated its commitment to raising the attainment of the bottom 20 per cent of pupils, bringing this closer to the average. Operating effective inclusion policies is seen as a key means of doing this. Despite this official endorsement, inclusion has not been without its critics, and an anti-inclusion backlash may be discerned both north and south of the Border. In this chapter, the evolution of thinking about inclusion is sketched, some of the reasons for conceptual confusion are outlined, and ways of measuring inclusion are explored. Finally, suggestions are made about future directions for conceptualising, operationalising and measuring inclusion.

Conceptualising inclusion

As noted in Chapter 1, there has always been some tension between the drive to create more specialist provision for children with SEN and the desire to include as many children as possible in mainstream schools. Drives for inclusive policies have always been influenced by budgetary considerations, since special schools with favourable teacher–pupil ratios are very expensive. On the other hand, providing high levels of support to children with SEN in mainstream classes is also expensive, since peripatetic support staff must be paid for. At the same time, social inclusion policies have led to the rejection of segregated forms of provision, whether these take the form of long-stay hospitals or special schools.

The Warnock Report (DES, 1978) provided a very strong endorsement of the principle of integration, referring to it as 'the central contemporary issue in special education'. Warnock argued:

> The principle of educating handicapped and non-handicapped children together, which is described as 'integration' in this country and 'mainstreaming' in the United States of America, and is recognised as a much wider movement of 'normalisation' in Scandinavia and Canada, is the particular expression of a widely held and still growing conviction that, as far as is humanly possible, handicapped people should share the opportunities for self-fulfilment enjoyed by other people. (p. 99, para 7.1)

Despite this support for integration, special schools were seen by the Warnock Committee as offering positive educational experiences to some disabled children as a result of favourable resourcing arrangements.

With regard to the principle of choice, Warnock promoted the idea of partnership with parents in pursuit of the child's best interests. The report did not embrace fully the notion of parent as final arbiter of appropriate educational provision and was criticised by commentators such as Kirp (1982) for failing to endorse a rights approach and reinforcing the principle of professional discretion. Overall, Warnock represented a cautious compromise, supporting partnership with parents but failing to challenge professionals' ultimate control over decision-making. Similarly, whilst endorsing the principle of integration, the ongoing role of special schools was affirmed.

In conceptualising integration, Warnock made a distinction between locational, social and functional integration. Locational integration (now referred to as mainstreaming) describes a situation where children with SEN were educated on the same site as other children, but tended to receive most of their education in a special unit. Social integration is used to describe a higher level of contact between the disabled child and others, so that all children spend recreation and lunch periods together, but might otherwise be educated separately for much of the time. The term functional integration is used to refer to a situation where a disabled children spends his or her entire school day in a mainstream setting. Whilst receiving additional support, the child follows essentially the same curriculum as other children in the class. Warnock's distinction has come to be regarded as too fixed and static. However, distinguishing between different types of integration is useful because it reminds us that, whilst the broad educational goals may be the same for all children, the precise targets and means of achieving these will be different. For example, it would be unreasonable to expect a child with complex difficulties to be taking three Highers. Whilst this may appear to be a rather obvious statement, some writing in this area seems to imply that all children should have precisely the same learning goals at all times.

As noted in Chapter 1, a rather different balance was called for by the Scottish HMI (SED, 1978), who argued for a much stronger commitment to the integration of children with learning difficulties into mainstream classes. Indeed, in the view of HMI, withdrawing children into segregated remedial classes tended to accentuate rather than alleviate their difficulties and distract attention from the central source of problems, the curriculum in mainstream schools. In this document, the principle of integration was seen as more important than the individual parent's right to choose their child's educational placement.

Yet another variation on the balance between the principles of integration and choice was struck by the 1980 Education (Scotland) Act (as amended). This legislation made no mention of educating children with SEN in mainstream classes, although provision for parental choice of school was extended to parents of children with SEN. It was assumed that parents who wished to do so would choose to have their children educated in a mainstream school. A range of caveats restricted the extent to which parents were able to exercise choices. If unreasonable additional expense were to be incurred by placing a child in a mainstream school, or the placement might be detrimental to the education of other children, then a parent's request for a mainstream placement could be refused. Integration was not seen as an essential component of the system, but as an option to be taken up if it accorded with parental wishes and if the authority was able to resource it. If provision were to move in this direction, then parental choice had to be the engine of change in accordance with market principles. At this stage, the child's preferences were not seen as a major deciding factor.

Subsequently, the discourse of integration was replaced by the discourse of inclusion. Corbett and Slee (2000), for example, drew a distinction between integration and inclusion. Integration was described as 'inherently assimilationist', forcing learners to fit into a uni-cultural 'mono-dimensional' mainstream. Inclusion, on the other hand, was seen as essentially transformative, fundamentally challenging 'existing hierarchies of status and privilege'. Armstrong *et al.* (2000a) described integration and inclusion as 'two opposing political goals'. Noting the establishment of this dichotomy between integration and inclusion, Booth (2000) suggested that attempts to see integration as synonymous with assimilation and inclusion as synonymous with transformation was an example of formulaic thinking which served to confuse, rather than clarify, the issue.

In support of this contention, Booth noted that early writing on integration, including the rather mild suggestions of the Warnock Committee, were regarded as extremely radical and threatening by the special education establishment who feared an attack on special schools. Sally Tomlinson's work on the sociology of special education (Tomlinson, 1982) was criticised by academics located within the educational psychology tradition, who considered that critical analysis of the grounds on which children were selected for 'special educational treatment' implied a rejection of the need for any additional support.

Booth also noted that, whilst some writing in the 'integration' tradition had quite radical implications, some work which espoused principles of inclusion was actually quite conservative in its implications. For example, the Tomlinson Report on *Inclusive Learning* (Tomlinson, 1997) defined inclusion as 'matching the resources we have to the learning styles and educational needs of the students'. In fairness, it should be noted that the report was about further education, where the diversity of the student population and the vocational mission of the sector make inclusion very difficult. Nonetheless, this definition is extremely minimalist, saying nothing about where young people with SEN should be educated and the extent to which high-level educational goals should be common to all. The idea of 'needs' is treated as unproblematic, although it appears that these will be defined by educators and reflect what is deliverable without the need for major change.

Finally, Booth drew attention to the fact that, whilst the UK government places a great deal of emphasis on its social inclusion agenda, this often fails to connect with the education of children with SEN. In Scotland, greater efforts have been made to link school inclusion with the wider social inclusion agenda. For example, the document *Special Educational Needs in Scotland* (Scottish Office, 1998, para 7) stated:

> An inclusive society must ensure that the potential of each individual is fully developed through education and that their attainment and achievement are valued and respected. It is on the realisation of this potential that inclusiveness depends; an inclusive society and education system will therefore strive to ensure that it creates the range of approaches and opportunities to ensure that this is brought about.

Similar views were expressed in the Scottish Parliament's *Report on the Inquiry into Special Educational Needs* (Scottish Parliament Education,

Culture and Sport Committee, 2001). Despite the widespread endorsement of inclusion, most official documents acknowledge the need for some form of segregated provision. Whilst the Learning Disabilities Review *The Same as You?* (Scottish Executive, 2000a) stated that fewer children with learning disabilities should be educated in segregated settings, the government's 29 social justice milestones do not include targets to do with the inclusion of disabled children (Scottish Executive, 2000b).

To summarise, inclusion may appear, on the face of it, to be a more radical concept than integration, but there is no agreement about an operational definition. As a result, it is possible for a wide range of practices to be described as inclusive and the absence of clear definition of inclusion makes it difficult to know to what extent it is being achieved.

Are Scottish schools becoming more inclusive?
In order to address this question, it is necessary to examine official statistics on the placement of children with special or additional support needs over time. The Scottish Executive conducts an annual schools census which collects data on all pupils in schools. The number and location of pupils with records of needs and/or IEPs in particular authorities is recorded by schools, as well as their principal learning difficulty. However, the data are difficult to interpret, partly because there are no firm criteria for opening a record of needs or an IEP, which has led to variation in local practice over many years. There has always been cross-authority variation in the proportion of children with a record of needs. In 2000, for example, the Scottish average was about 2 per cent; the lowest recording authority was East Dunbartonshire, formally identifying about 0.8 per cent, and the highest recording authority was Inverclyde, identifying almost 3 per cent of the school population. The criteria for opening a record of needs and/or an IEP are essentially relativistic, that is, a child is deemed to require additional support if their needs are greater than those of other children in a similar environment. Therefore it is unsurprising that local differences in identifying additional support needs have persisted and in some authorities have become even more marked. As illustrated in Table 6, about 4 per cent of children in primary and secondary schools have a record of needs and/or an IEP. At primary level, this varies from 1.5 per cent in Glasgow to 9.8 per cent in Shetland. At secondary level, the range is even greater, varying from 1.2 per cent in North Ayrshire to 11.4 per cent in Dundee. Whilst normative impairments such as blindness occur across the population fairly randomly, there is a strong association between social disadvantage and the occurrence of non-normative conditions such as moderate learning difficulties and behavioural difficulties. It is therefore slightly surprising that an authority such as Glasgow, with very high levels of deprivation, has such a low proportion of records of needs and IEPs. Dundee, on the other hand, with

Table 6: Primary, secondary and special school pupils with a Record of Needs (RoN) and/or an Individualised Educational Programme (IEP), 2005

	All pupils in primary schools with RoN and/or IEP	% of all primary pupils with RoN/ IEP	All pupils in secondary schools with RoN and/or IEP
Scotland	15,519	4.0	12,014
Aberdeen City	425	3.3	222
Aberdeenshire	1,151	5.8	913
Angus	370	4.1	158
Argyll & Bute	224	3.3	263
Clackmannanshire	134	3.3	160
Dumfries & Galloway	716	6.3	402
Dundee City	619	6.9	962
East Ayrshire	569	5.9	309
East Dunbartonshire	174	1.9	124
East Lothian	164	2.1	97
East Renfrewshire	246	2.9	203
Edinburgh	949	3.7	662
Eilean Siar	190	8.9	81
Falkirk	723	6.0	510
Fife	926	3.3	957
Glasgow City	609	1.5	464
Highland	785	4.5	600
Inverclyde	310	4.9	303
Midlothian	257	3.9	177
Moray	314	4.2	259
North Ayrshire	281	2.5	109
North Lanarkshire	579	2.1	475
Orkney Islands	91	5.6	63
Perth & Kinross	750	7.3	509
Renfrewshire	497	3.7	451
Scottish Borders	327	3.8	375
Shetland Islands	191	9.8	158
South Ayrshire	644	7.9	558
South Lanarkshire	1,118	4.6	714
Stirling	221	3.2	210
West Dunbartonshire	197	2.7	151
West Lothian	688	4.7	415

Source: Scottish Executive, 2006a

% of all secondary pupils with RoN/IEP	All pupils in special schools with RoN and/or IEP	% of all special school pupils with RoN/IEP	Number and % of all pupils with RoN/IEP in special schools	% of all school pupils in special settings
3.8	6,688	98.6	34,221 (19.5%)	1%
2.1	274	99.6	921 (30%)	1.17%
5.8	243	100	2,307 (10.5%)	0.68%
2.2	#	#	528 (0%)	0%
4.6	44	100	531 (8.2%)	0.35%
5.3	37	100	331 (0%)	0.52%
4.2	12	100	1,130 (1.06%)	0.08%
11.4	119	100	1,700 (7.0%)	0.64%
3.8	177	100	1,055 (16.7%)	0.98%
1.5	157	98.1	455 (34.5%)	0.91%
1.7	–	#	261 (0%)	0%
2.6	52	100	762 (6.8%)	0.32%
3.3	732	100	2,343 (31.2%)	1.6%
4.3	#	#	271 (0%)	0%
5.6	192	100	1,425 (13.5%)	0.90%
4.3	147	100	1,130 (13.0%)	0.29%
1.6	1,818	98.6	2,891 (62.8%)	2.64%
4.0	174	100	1,559 (0%)	0.53%
5.6	131	100	744 (17.6%)	1.10%
3.2	107	64.8	541 (19.8%)	1.34%
4.3	#	#	573 (0%)	0%
1.2	163	97.6	553 (29.4%)	0.82%
2.1	764	100	1,818 (42%)	1.5%
4.4	#	#	154 (0%)	0%
6.3	53	100	1,312 (4.0%)	0.29%
3.9	299	100	1,247 (24.0%)	1.18%
5.4	–	#	702 (0%)	0%
9.4	#	#	349 (0%)	0%
7.6	89	100	1,291 (6.9%)	0.57%
3.5	515	100	2,347 (22%)	1.14%
3.5	34	100	465 (7.3%)	0.26%
2.4	125	100	473 (26.4%)	0.9%
3.8	230	100	1,333 (17.2%)	0.88%

similarly high levels of deprivation, identifies a relatively high proportion of children as having additional support needs, particularly at secondary level. A further surprising finding from Table 6 is that some children in special schools do not have a record of needs and/or an IEP, given that, by virtue of their placement, these children have been identified as having additional support needs. In Midlothian, for example, about a third of children in special schools do not have a record of needs or an IEP.

Having noted the relative nature of the criteria used to identify children with additional support needs, and the variations in practice which this produces, let us now consider the extent to which the data reveal changes over time in patterns of inclusion. As noted in Table 7, the proportion of children identified with additional support needs has increased over the past four years, rising from about 3 per cent to 4 per cent in primary school, with a slightly lower proportion being identified in secondary. This reflects the less stringent criteria for the creation of an IEP, which are much less stringent than for the opening of a record of needs. As discussed more fully in Chapter 5, whereas the IEP is intended to establish and monitor targets for teaching and learning, the record of needs, as least in its initial conception, was intended to identify the child's difficulties and the measures proposed by the local authority to meet their additional needs. The increase in the proportion of children identified as having additional support needs is explained, therefore, not by a greater incidence of disability and difficulty, but rather by the move to a broader understanding of what counts as an

Table 7: Pupils with a Record of Needs and/or an Individualised Educational Programme in mainstream schools, primary and secondary, 2002–2005

	Primary	Secondary						
	2002	**2003**	2004	2005	2002	2003	2004	2005
All the time in mainstream classes	10,618	11,514	12,452	13,246	6,134	7,324	8,547	9,542
Some time spent in mainstream classes	1,406	1,749	1,731	1,852	1,741	1,998	1,881	2,027
No time in mainstream classes	287	319	386	423	332	362	366	450
Total	12,311	13,582	14,569	15,521	8,207	9,684	10,794	12,019
Percentage of school roll	3.0	3.3	3.7	4.0	2.6	3.0	3.4	3.8

Source: Scottish Executive, 2006a

additional support need. Entirely consistent with this shift in understanding of additional support needs is the move, as noted in Figure 1, to educate a higher proportion of children with additional support needs in mainstream schools. Intriguingly, Figure 1 shows that whilst there has been a marked increase in the number of children with additional support needs spending all of their time in mainstream classes, there has also been a small increase in the number spending only some of their time in mainstream classes or spending all of their time is special classes. On the basis of this evidence, one would have to conclude that there has been an increase in the number and proportion of children with additional support needs in mainstream classes, but this is largely explained by the expanded definition of additional support needs, and, following from this, the increase in the number of children with additional support needs whose difficulties are less significant.

Figure 1: Pupils with a Record of Needs and/or an Individualised Educational Programme in mainstream schools, primary and secondary, 2002-2005

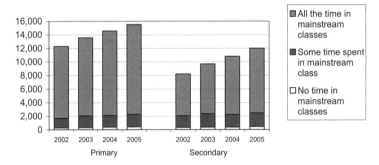

Source: Scottish Executive, 2006a

Figure 2: Pupil numbers by sector, 1996–2005

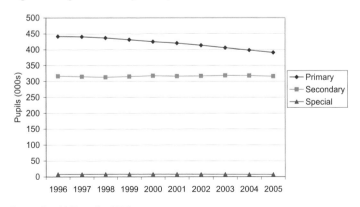

Source: Scottish Executive, 2006a

A further measure of the extent of inclusion is the proportion of the school population in special schools and units (see Figure 2). Whilst there has been a fall in the school population in line with a general population decline, there has been only a very small decline in the proportion of pupils in special settings.

Indeed, as demonstrated by Table 8, whilst the number of pupils in special settings has declined, the number of special schools has increased.

Table 8: Schools and pupils in publicly funded special schools, 1997–2005

	Schools	Girls	Boys	Total
1997	158	2,872	5,184	8,056
1998	185	2,885	5,346	8,231
1999	195	2,871	5,440	8,311
2000	195	2,847	5,471	8,318
2001	197	2,755	5,428	8,183
2002	191	2,605	5,376	7,981
2003	194	2,531	5,149	7,680
2004	192	2,381	5,008	7,389
2005	190	2,302	4,838	7,140

Source: Scottish Executive, 2006a

The explanation for the apparent growth in the number of schools accompanied by the declining number of pupils is explained by the closure of some large special schools, and the shift to a greater number of special units. However, the Scottish Executive Statistical Bulletin notes the need for caution in interpreting these figures, since some schools count children with additional support needs in special units attached to mainstream as being in mainstream schools. The issue of what counts as a special setting is thus becoming increasingly hazy.

Whilst the use of special schools has been remarkably constant, it is also clear that there is considerable diversity across different local authorities in their use of special schools (see Table 6). Authorities making high use of special schools include Glasgow (2.6 per cent) and Edinburgh (1.6 per cent). Rural authorities, on the other hand, often have no special schools, and authorities which were part of the former Strathclyde and Lothian regions until regional reorganisation in 1996 also tend to make less use of special settings since historically children requiring a special placement might be sent to Edinburgh or Glasgow. Although it appears that some authorities do not educate any children in special settings, this is because they purchase places for children in neighbouring authorities, independent special schools or grant aided schools. All authorities, in reality, use the special sector to a greater or lesser extent.

To summarise, because the criteria for having a record of needs or an IEP have never been clearly defined and are relative to the context in which the child is being educated, the statistics are difficult to interpret. However, there is no evidence to support the view that large numbers of children who would previously have been educated in the special sector are now in mainstream schools. Nonetheless, some of the trends noted here might benefit from closer scrutiny. For example, a number of authorities appear to be identifying fewer children with additional support needs (i.e. having a record of needs or an IEP). These authorities include North Ayrshire, East Dunbartonshire, North Lanarkshire, Glasgow, East Lothian, West Dunbartonshire and Aberdeen City. This variation is unlikely to be as a result of differing incidence, but is much more likely to be based on local beliefs that children will be catered for adequately in mainstream schools and individual planning is not necessary. However, issues of accountability, equity and rights arise here. As noted in Chapters 3 and 4, in Scotland there are different means for parents to seek redress in the field of additional support needs, and the most transparent route to justice, the Additional Support Needs Tribunal, is only available to a small number who meet tightly defined criteria. Alternative dispute resolution through adjudication or mediation is a possibility, but may not deliver redress and may serve the purpose of reaching agreement by attrition. As discussed earlier, schools in the past sometimes encouraged parents to request a record of needs in order to obtain additional resources for the school. If schools perceive that no additional resource is attached to a pupil whom they perceive as being difficult to educate, then their enthusiasm for inclusion may be dampened. This is a point we return to in the subsequent discussion on the backlash against inclusion.

Other means of exclusion

Overall, the category of additional support needs has expanded and a greater proportion of children with additional support needs are now being mainstreamed; in other words, they are not attending special schools. However, almost one-third of these children are not always in mainstream classes (Scottish Executive, 2006a), and the use of special settings has not markedly declined. Spatial exclusion – if not educational and social exclusion – is therefore experienced by a good number of children and the policy discourse has always been ambivalent in this regard. Ministers and official pronouncements have been careful to promote inclusion in general but retain the possibility of specialist, spatially-segregated provision. The concerns of parents who want specialist provision for their children, and the fears of long-established specialist providers, lead to political sensitivities in relation to disbanding segregated provision.

Placement in special schools, units or bases is, however, only one means of educating children outwith mainstream classes. Despite the introduction and subsequent removal of exclusion targets, school exclusions have risen over recent years. Indeed, the latest figures for 2004/05 (Scottish Executive, 2006b) show a higher number of exclusions (41,974) than the target baseline set by the social justice agenda of 34,831 in 1998/99. Following representations from teacher unions and head teachers, the Scottish Executive announced in 2004 that they would no longer be proceeding with the target for reducing school exclusion. Social class differentials are evident, so that a disproportionate number of children eligible for free school meals (a proxy for socio-economic disadvantage) and those who are looked after by the state are identified as having additional support needs and are excluded from school (Scottish Executive, 2006b).

Figure 3: Number of pupils with free school meals, RoN / IEP, and looked after by local authority, 2005[1]

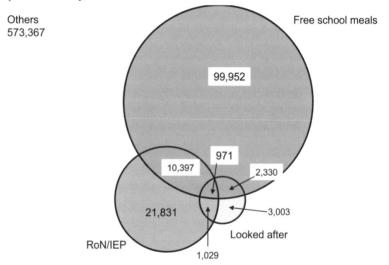

[1] Data does not include grant aided special schools.
Source: Scottish Executive, 2006a

These data can be interpreted in different ways. On the one hand, there have been concerns that children who are looked after by the state are not having their additional support needs recognised, perhaps because local authorities are not acting as 'good parents' in taking forward the assessment procedures (Borland *et al.* 1998), and similar concerns have been expressed in relation to children living in poverty. This line of argument would suggest that an even higher proportion of looked after children should be formally identified and provided with additional support. On the other hand, disproportionate identification of certain groups might lead to their social stigmatisation, and it is certainly the case that looked after children and those entitled to free school meals are significantly more likely to be excluded from school (Scottish Executive, 2006b).

Boys are more likely than girls to be identified as having additional support needs, excluded from school and placed in special schools and units. In 2005, 70 per cent of pupils with additional support needs, 68 per cent of pupils attending special schools and 79 per cent of those excluded from schools were male (Scottish Executive, 2006a; 2006b). These differences may well relate to a greater identification of boys as having particular impairments than girls: for example, in such categories as social, emotional and behavioural difficulties (SEBD), autistic spectrum disorder, and moderate learning difficulties (Scottish Executive, 2006a). Gender differentials are not always negative for boys. For example, more boys are likely to be categorised as having specific learning difficulties (71 per cent of this category (Scottish Executive, 2006a)) and this may give them assistance of scribes or readers and (possibly) lower university entrance level requirements (Riddell *et al.*, 2005). In general, however, despite attracting additional resources, boys tend to be penalised rather than assisted by their increased tendency to be identified with additional support needs, since this is associated with a higher risk of exclusion.

The backlash against inclusion

Official policy statements endorse inclusion, whilst continuing to see a place for the special sector. However, it is evident that there is a growing tide of opinion both north and south of the Border that inclusion has 'gone too far' and that there is a need to create additional provision for children with emotional and behavioural difficulties. Many teacher concerns around inclusion appear to stem not so much from the inclusion of pupils with physical or sensory impairments, but rather relate to a perception of a rising tide of indiscipline and violent behaviour by a growing group of children with social, emotional and behavioural difficulties. Munn *et al.* (2004) found that most teachers continued to report low-level indiscipline as their major concern, although a small but significant rise in violent incidents was also reported. This mood is reflected in a recent report produced by the Educational Institute of Scotland (EIS) entitled *Supporting Teachers, Tackling Indiscipline* (EIS, 2006), which states that:

> There is a growing recognition that the policy of inclusion is not working for many pupils who exhibit violent behaviour. Currently, however, there is a lack of suitable provision.

To address the problem of pupil indiscipline, the EIS argues for additional support targeted at individual pupils, more off-site units, a reiteration of a head teacher's right to exclude, and the instigation of a new category of permanent exclusion. In addition, there is a call for clearer discipline policies based on consultation with staff and stronger leadership. In England, following an intervention by Mary Warnock, there appear to be additional concerns about the inclusion of children with autistic spectrum disorder, and the mission of protecting special schools has become a party-political issue championed by the Conservatives. Arguments about inclusion versus special schooling tend to be data-free, and, as indicated above, the evidence, although somewhat complex, does not support a wholesale abandonment of placement outwith the mainstream, but, if anything, an increase in spatial exclusion.

Why are inclusive policies so difficult to implement?

A somewhat paradoxical situation exists, therefore, in which there is strong official endorsement of educational inclusion, but very little shared knowledge about how this is to be achieved and how success may be assessed. In the following sections, some possible explanations of the difficulties encountered in implementing inclusive policies are explored.

Tensions between inclusion and choice

In Scotland there appears to be a consensus around the position that, whilst mainstream placement may be the preferred option, various forms of specialist provision will be needed into the foreseeable future and certainly no target has been set for the closure of special schools. One reason for this is the emphasis on parental choice following the publication of *The Parents' Charter for Scotland* (Scottish Office, 1991). Whilst marketisation and consumerism were never as well developed in Scotland as in England, the personalisation of public services is a key theme for the Labour–Liberal coalition administration at Holyrood, and therefore removing choice from consumers of public services would be seen as undesirable, particularly in such a sensitive area.

The disability movement also continues to hedge its bets in this area. Segregated provision has been identified as one of the major factors reinforcing the inferiority of disabled children (see, for example, the accounts of Barnes, 1991 and Mason, 1993). Moves towards entirely inclusive systems of education are evident in some parts of the developed world. For example, in Canada the existence of special classes has been challenged under provincial Human Rights Codes and the Canadian Charter of Rights and Freedoms. Inclusion has been seen as a 'pressing human rights issue', and the segregation of disabled children in special schools has been compared with the historical segregation of black people. However, some disabled people themselves argue for certain forms of separate specialist provision. Corker (1998), for example, describes the historical tensions between Deaf culture and the disability movement, as deaf people struggle to achieve cultural autonomy based on the use of sign language. People who identify with Deaf culture see themselves not as disabled, but as a linguistic minority requiring sign-language medium education just as some Gaelic-speakers argue for Gaelic medium education. Other groups, such as blind people, may defend the principle of separate school systems where Braille may be taught to academically able blind children. The fact that the disability movement has discovered deep internal divisions in relation to inclusive education has made it difficult to hold a simple and consistent position.

Tensions between individualised and systemic approaches
The development of special needs education has been informed by the idea that a small group of children require individually crafted provision to assist them in learning. Special schools have traditionally had much better teacher–pupil ratios and specialist equipment, and some parents believe that their child's individual needs are best served in this type of environment. An alternative approach is to argue for a systemic approach to meeting children's additional support needs. Rather than emphasising individual assessments and programmes, the aim should be to make curriculum and pedagogy accessible for all. This is a view which is strongly endorsed by many professionals, and the Scottish Executive passed legislation (the Education (Disability Strategies and Pupils' Educational Records) (Scotland) Act 2002) which places a duty on local authorities to make the education they provide accessible (see Chapter 6 for further discussion). Individualised and systemic approaches tend to co-exist alongside each other (Tisdall and Riddell, 2006), and again there are fears that downplaying the importance of supporting the individual child in favour of systemic change would produce a negative political reaction from parents and voluntary organisations.

Tensions between curriculum entitlement
and the developmental curriculum
Special schools are often seen as places where there can be considerable freedom around what is taught and how it is taught, in contrast with mainstream schools where worries about meeting the goals of the national curriculum overshadow other concerns. When the 5–14 Curriculum in Scotland and the National Curriculum in England were introduced, there was considerable ambivalence about their relevance to pupils with SEN. It was argued by some that for children with severe and profound learning difficulties, who would be largely focusing on developmental matters, there was little point in participating in a common curriculum and assessment framework. Others, such as Heward and Lloyd-Smith (1990) and Hegarty (1989), argued that children with SEN had much to gain from being included in a national curriculum and assessment framework. Practitioners, it was suggested, would be forced to think much more carefully about teaching and assessment methods. In addition, parents had a right to accessible

information about educational targets and progress. In England, a formal system was put in place for the 'disapplication' of the National Curriculum and assessment, but was rarely used. In both England and Scotland, special needs teachers were encouraged to find ways of customising the national curriculum to make it accessible to children with additional support needs. However, such efforts do not appear to have been an unalloyed success, and arguments for special schools have therefore persisted on the basis of the curricular freedom which they are seen as facilitating.

Tensions around differentiating the curriculum
If children with additional support needs are to be taught successfully in mainstream settings, then teachers have to invest time and energy in preparing a differentiated curriculum. However, international research (OECD, 2005) and experience in Scotland suggest that, in general, teachers find the task of differentiation difficult and time-consuming, and would rather pass over responsibility for children with additional support needs to the learning support teacher. Progress on curriculum differentiation was also hindered by the lack of published research on how to improve the learning and teaching of children with additional educational needs in mainstream settings. Recent work compiled by Wearmouth (2001) has highlighted a number of effective of classroom strategies, such as explicitly teaching the rules for effective small group interaction (Mercer, 2001), the application of peer tutoring techniques (Merrett, 2001), and the incorporation of therapy into the mainstream curriculum (Pickles, 2001). Meanwhile, debates continue about whether children with additional support needs require a curriculum and pedagogy which is essentially similar to, or different from, that which is generally taught (Lewis and Norwich, 2005). Arguments for specialist curricula often imply that specialist settings with groups of similar children are preferable, whereas mainstream settings tend to be promoted by those who maintain that the curriculum and pedagogy are essentially the same for all learners, albeit with significant adaptations for some pupils.

Conclusion
This chapter has described the gradual development of inclusive educational policies over time, and has highlighted some of the difficulties in discerning the extent of progress which has been made towards realising the goal of inclusion. The complexity of the statistics was highlighted, and it was argued that, although there is a popular perception that a great deal (and possibly too much) progress has been made towards inclusion, the available data do not fully support this conclusion. Whilst there has been an expansion in the category of additional support needs, leading to apparently greater numbers of children with additional support needs being included in mainstream, the proportion of children placed in special settings has altered very little

over a long period of time, and the number of special units has increased. It is evident that significant numbers of children continue to be spatially segregated, and there are strong associations with dimensions of social disadvantage and underachievement, including entitlement to free school meals and being looked after by the local authority, the negative effects of which are amplified for boys. The chapter concluded by outlining some of the tensions around inclusion, which explain why the translation of the policy into practice has been somewhat muted. To clarify this slightly opaque picture, ongoing analysis of statistics over time is required, as well as qualitative work to illuminate the extent to which inclusive practices are being incorporated into the everyday life of schools. In particular, the effectiveness of additional support staff, and the quality of differentiated pedagogy, requires closer examination.

Chapter 5

SOCIAL INCLUSION AND RAISING STANDARDS: COMPETING AGENDAS IN THE FIELD OF ADDITIONAL SUPPORT NEEDS

Introduction

For at least a decade and a half, there has been a growing concern to ensure the accountability of public services including education. Whereas the previous Conservative administration's focus on accountability was fuelled by a belief that the public sector was prone to inefficiency, Scottish and UK New Labour administrations have attempted to link the raising standards agenda with the school inclusion and social justice agendas. This chapter explores the nature of accountability policies in relation to SEN and presents findings from a Scottish Executive funded research project on a national initiative which attempted to monitor the attainment of targets set within IEPs for children with SEN (Banks *et al.*, 2001).

Accountability and audit in the public sector

By the 1980s, groups from the left and the right were making the case for the reform of the public sector. Dissatisfaction with the quality and responsiveness of public services was driven in part by the growing demands of service users for more individually-tailored rather than standardised services. These dissatisfactions were exploited by the new right, which suggested that much tighter management was needed to ensure value for money, efficiency and effectiveness. A new managerialist approach was advocated, informed by the ideas of US liberal economists such as von Hayek, who argued that the welfare state should be no more than a safety net for those in greatest need. According to Pollitt (1993), the central thesis of those promoting new public management was that all human activity, particularly that associated with the workplace, could and should be measured, and that this was the basis of effective management. Tight audit procedures were required to ensure the delivery of value for money and to guard against the self-serving tendencies of public sector professionals and workers.

Prime Minister James Callaghan, in his Ruskin College speech of 1976, signalled his government's dissatisfaction with school performance and, had the Labour Party been elected in 1979, it would almost certainly have sought to increase public sector accountability through the audit of school and local authority performance. Instead, the election of a Conservative government in that year led to the adoption of a new right version of public sector management closely wedded to the wider policy goal of public sector marketisation. From the start of the Conservative administration's third term of office in 1987, the reform of education moved to centre stage and the application of private sector management principles was identified as the central means of infusing education with a competitive, market-orientated ethos (Deakin, 1994). As reflected in the recent White Paper *Modernising Government* (Cabinet Office, 1999), the Westminster and Holyrood administrations have further developed the audit culture (Power, 1997) establishing Best Value as the governing regime of all public services and promoting a mixed economy of welfare, with services delivered by the public, private and voluntary sectors. This promotion of the voluntary and private sector, along with the transfer of cash to purchase services directly, has gone much further in relation to community care, where direct payments have been described by some government ministers as the default form of service provision (Riddell *et al.*, 2005).

Despite the policy continuities of the Conservative and New Labour governments, the underpinning discourse of public accountability has shifted, with New Labour distancing itself from the Conservative's neoliberal objectives and attempting to use audit technologies as a means of modernising the welfare state (Fergusson, 2000). However, the overall impact of the growing centrality of audit and accountability continues to be debated. Some commentators have suggested that accountability regimes may have different purposes, methods and serve a range of political goals. For example, Fairley and Paterson (1995) distinguished between market, bureaucratic and democratic versions of accountability. Others, for instance Power (1997), suggested that the expansion of accountability and audit may be indicative of a breakdown of social trust and the effects of audit must be carefully monitored because of the tendency to produce a range of dysfunctional responses within organisations. One such response was described by Power as colonisation, and occurs when the goals of the organisation become taken over by the performance indicators which are assessed. As a result, the organisation loses sight of its own objectives and values.

An alternative response was described in terms of decoupling. When this takes place, an individual within the organisation takes on responsibility for audit compliance, whilst others continue to pursue their independent goals. Whereas Power accepted that evaluation, assessment, checking and account-giving are part of everyday human interaction, he maintained that an uncritical belief in the efficacy of accountability regimes may produce 'deluded visions of control and transparency which are neither as effective nor as neutral as commonly imagined' (Power, 1997, p. 143). As noted above, this chapter uses the case of SEN to explore the extent to which the dual goals of raising standards and social inclusion are compatible and capable of being achieved through the application of managerialist accountability principles. Before considering the *Raising Standards in Special Educational Needs* initiative more closely, it is necessary to consider the history of accountability within Scottish education and the SEN system.

Scottish education and accountability

During the 1980s, accountability policies in Scotland, as in England, were driven by the increasingly radical agenda of the Conservative government, although this agenda tended to be implemented in a more muted form north of the Border. The *Parents' Charter for Scotland*, first published in 1991 and updated in 1995, emphasised the importance of quality, standards, information, choice and value for money. Within the model of accountability implicit in the Parents' Charter, service consumers, envisaged as parents rather than children, were seen as the drivers of reform, using readily accessible information to inform rational choices and use 'voice' to influence future policy direction. The (theoretical) outcome of consumerist and marketised principles was greater efficiency, effectiveness and value for money, since, in a social re-enactment of Darwinist principles, services which were poorly adapted to market conditions would wither and die, whilst the better adapted would survive and flourish.

Access to simple information was central to this vision of the empowered consumer. The Conservative government sought ways of providing such information, but the implementation of auditable systems was impeded by the government's tenuous political legitimacy, which meant that educational reform, whilst drawing from a common UK policy repertoire (McPherson and Raab, 1988), was implemented at a much slower pace. For example, the 5–14 programme (SOED, 1987), was introduced by regulation rather than law, unlike its English counterpart. There was strong resistance to national testing from both teachers and parents, on the grounds that formal assessment was likely to label some children as failures at a very early age and might undermine the principles of comprehensive schooling by creating a hierarchy of schools. As a result of a parental boycott, it was agreed that teachers should base their assessment of pupils on normal teaching activities, using items selected from a national assessment bank, and tests should be administered to individuals or groups of children merely to confirm teachers' judgements that a certain standard had been achieved. Education authorities would not gather or publish information on the tests, thus making league tables of primary schools impossible to compile. It should be noted, however, that standardised tests have subsequently been introduced by education authorities to provide accurate baseline assessment information, justified, in part, as a means of measuring the success of early intervention strategies.

Whilst there was reluctance to publish primary league tables in Scotland, regulations (SOED, 1992a) required schools to publish data on examination results, attendance, school leaver destinations, school costs and policy on SEN. Financial devolution to the school level (SOED, 1992b) was justified on the grounds that it empowered school managers to target resources on centrally identified performance indicators. A further boost to the accountability project was the establishment of an Audit Unit within the Inspectorate with the task of collecting, analysing and publishing evidence about the performance of schools and education departments. In addition to the publication of documents on standards and quality in Scottish schools based on inspections and performance indicators, the Audit Unit encouraged schools to engage in self-evaluation (SOEID, 1996b), suggesting that performance indicators identified by the school should be used to identify and monitor the achievement of specific, achievable and measurable targets. The implications of giving schools responsibility for their own improvement has been much debated (see, for example, the collection of papers edited by Riddell and Brown, 1991). Whereas commentators like Hargreaves (1990) concluded that schools cannot honestly evaluate themselves due to internal resistance to critical scrutiny, Stoll (1991) argued that school improvement is more likely to be achieved through professionals taking responsibility for their own work, rather than through the external imposition of centralised control.

The emphasis on schools taking responsibility for their own development, with a relatively 'light touch' being exerted by central and local government, accorded well with Scottish resistance to the marketisation of services and general suspicion of the motives of the Westminster government. Despite this endorsement of school self-evaluation as the central mechanism of school improvement, the Audit Unit issued warnings about the relatively poor performance of Scottish schools in international league tables and in 1996 the Conservative administration, as one of its last acts, established a Task Force on underachievement in Scottish schools (SOEID, 1996c).

The Task Force report was significant in arguing that a tighter audit regime was required to tackle educational inequality rather than to promote a market-driven agenda. It noted problems with basic literacy in disadvantaged areas and recommended that there should be a significant shift from internal school regulation to external accountability. Children's attainments in relation to the 5–14 programme should be reported to education authorities and placed in the public domain, a decisive shift from the earlier position where the school reported the individual child's results to parents. The Task Force endorsed the public reporting of external examination results, but favoured the use of value added data over crude league tables, a decisive shift from HMI's earlier position that taking account of pupil background was simply 'making excuses' for under-achievement. (See Riddell (1997) for discussion of the representation of social class in school effectiveness research.) Finally, the Task Force report commended the setting of targets as advocated by the Advisory Scottish Council for Education and Training Targets (ASCETT), drawing on human capital arguments:

> All industrialised nations are in the course of raising educational attainment across their populations. There is a widespread recognition that the quality of education is a major determinant of successful economic competitiveness. (SOEID, 1996c, p. 5)

The advent of a New Labour government at Westminster and a Labour–Liberal coalition government within the Scottish Parliament at Holyrood provided the conditions for new policy initiatives to emerge after the stalemate of the last years of the Conservative government. Given this opportunity for new beginnings, it is interesting that target-setting should emerge as New Labour's flagship policy (see, for example, the advisory document *Setting Targets – Raising Standards in Schools* (SOEID, 1998b) and the White Paper *Targeting Excellence: Modernising Scotland's Schools* (SOEID, 1999a). There was a strong degree of continuity between Conservative and New Labour education policies in terms of espousing new managerialist policies and practices. However, the justification of these policies was different; whilst both administrations emphasised value for money, the Conservatives promoted consumer choice whilst, for New Labour, social inclusion was the dominant discourse.

The Education (Standards in Scotland's Schools etc.) (Scotland) Act 2000 provided the legislative backing for the rigorous, quantifiable and public forms of accountability signalled in the earlier policy papers. Scottish Ministers and education authorities were given the responsibility to 'secure improvement in the quality of school education' and a direct duty was placed on government to identify performance indicators for Scottish education and provide independent, external evaluation of the education functions of local authorities (Scottish Executive, 1999, p. 15). Education authorities were given a duty to prepare a statement of improvement objectives in the areas of national priority identified by Scottish Ministers and put in place arrangements to ensure they identify and take action to continuously improve performance in schools (Scottish Executive, 1999, p. 16). It is now established practice for local authorities to set targets for each school to achieve annually, and, for children with SEN, performance in relation to targets specified on the IEP is a central part of this assessment.

To summarise, the Scottish Office, and subsequently the Scottish Executive, consistently promoted a managerialist agenda informed by a market-driven and consumerist version of accountability. However, the Conservative government's lack of political legitimacy in Scotland meant that a centrally-controlled audit culture was slower to take hold and ran alongside a system based on professional self-regulation. New Labour, having greater political credibility in Scotland partly as a result of its constitutional reforms, intensified educational audit regimes, whilst favouring bureaucratic rather than market-based versions of accountability with social inclusion as the legitimating discourse. Whilst the Scottish Parliament declared its opposition to the publication of primary league tables, local newspapers have published primary and secondary school league tables based on existing data.

Special educational needs policy in Scotland and accountability
As argued in earlier chapters of this book, educational accountability has been looser in Scotland than in England, particularly in relation to children with SEN. Revised arrangements for national testing, published in 1992, stated that pupils with SEN and those for whom English was not their first language should only be assessed when they had reached level A. These children, it was argued, could not be assessed using existing instruments and the preparation of specialised tests would be too time-consuming and expensive. Responsibility for the education of children with SEN, it was argued, should continue to reside with the professionals, who would determine what to teach and whether pupils were making progress.

Whilst some SEN professionals welcomed the freedom from the 5–14 programme, other interest groups, including members of the disability movement, pointed out that teachers of disabled children were less accountable than others. In 1993, HMI issued advice on the adaptation of the 5–14 programme for children with SEN (SOED, 1993), recommending broad approaches to the curriculum rather than attempting to benchmark knowledge and skills. The publication *Effective Provision for Special Educational Needs* (EPSEN) (SOED, 1994) attempted to specify management principles to ensure quality and standards. Special schools and units were advised to produce development plans and report progress in achieving identified goals on a three-year cycle. Whilst imposing some degree of external accountability, the onus lay with the school to identify institutional targets, establish success criteria and evaluate progress. A higher degree of external accountability was signalled in the growing emphasis on Individualised Educational Programmes, which were variously described as a means of charting the individual child's progress, identifying the educational provision to be made by the school in conjunction with the record of needs, or evaluating the school's effectiveness in relation to aggregating targets achieved by individual children. The first two functions of the IEP were not new, since gearing teaching towards children's individual needs has a long history within special needs education. However, the idea that teachers and schools might be held accountable for the achievement of learning goals was very radical.

Having established the general principle of accountability, subsequent advice (e.g. *Raising Standards – Setting Targets: Targets for Pupils with Special Educational Needs* (SOEID, 1999b), specified audit mechanisms in more detail. After a pilot year in academic session 1999–2000, special schools and units, as well as mainstream schools educating pupils with SEN, were required to report to the Scottish Executive all learning goals set for children with SEN and the proportion of targets achieved. Schools were advised that IEPs should be opened for all children in special schools and units and all children with records of needs in mainstream schools. In addition, all children in mainstream schools without a record of needs but requiring 'significant planned intervention' should have an IEP. Targets should be set in one or more of the following curriculum areas: communication and language; numeracy; personal and social development. The number of long-term targets to be achieved during the course of a school sessions could range from 1–2 targets within one area of the curriculum to 8–12 or more targets across three areas of the curriculum. The long-term targets for each pupil were to be broken down into about four short-term targets, each of which should be covered in 6–8 weeks. The targets were to be SMART (specific, measurable, achievable, relevant and timely). They might be based on qualitative or quantitative data, and success criteria and evidence should be stipulated at the outset. Deciding whether a target had been achieved would depend, to a greater or lesser extent, on professional judgement. At the end of each school session, the achievement of long-term targets should be recorded and new targets set. At the end of the academic year, aggregated data were to be reported to the Scottish Executive. In schools with a significant number of pupils with SEN, 80 per cent of pupils were expected to achieve 80 per cent of targets. In schools with a small number of pupils with SEN, each pupil was expected to achieve 80 per cent of his or her individual targets. The advice to schools acknowledged that:

> Some pupils with very complex needs and health-related difficulties may show very small incremental changes in a year and may well become less responsive. (SOEID, 1999b, p. 40, para 7)

Nonetheless, all pupils, no matter how significant their needs, were to be included in the target-setting programme. As well as having their IEP target outcomes reported to the Scottish Executive, pupils with SEN were also to be included in the mainstream target-setting exercise. According to the Scottish Executive, unless children with SEN were included in the mainstream accountability initiative, this would be seen as anti-inclusive. Some head teachers expressed concerns that that this might militate against the inclusion of disabled children in mainstream schools, but this argument was not accepted by the Scottish Executive, who said that mainstream targets could be adjusted to reflect the proportion of children with SEN. However, there was a general lack of clarity about which children were to be included or excluded.

The target-setting initiative was phased in, with only schools which considered they were ready being fully involved in the first phase, from April 1999 to the end of session 1999/2000. More schools joined in August 1999. From April 2000, all schools were expected to collate information derived from pupil reviews and individual planning meetings in order to develop statements of long-term targets with appropriate success criteria. By August 2000, all schools were expected to have set targets and have systems in place to track progress.

The research project

The project *Raising Standards for Pupils with Special Educational Needs*, commissioned by the Scottish Executive Education Department, ran from January 2000 to February 2001. It was undertaken jointly by researchers from the Strathclyde Centre for Disability Research and the St Andrew's Faculty of Education at the University of Glasgow and the Special Educational Needs Research Centre at the University of Newcastle. The aims of the research were:

- to identify examples of the effective use of IEPs in special schools and units;
- to compare this with the use of IEPs with a small sample of children with SEN in mainstream education;
- to explore the relationship between IEPs and raising attainment; and
- to make recommendations for the effective use of IEPs.

The methods used consisted of a literature review, key informant interviews, a questionnaire survey of all special schools and units and a sample of mainstream primary and secondary schools, and case studies of the use of IEPs with children with a range of learning difficulties in mainstream and special settings at primary and secondary levels. Full details of the research are reported in Banks *et al.* (2001). As indicated above, the main concern of this chapter is to explore the implications of strengthening accountability in relation to children with SEN and the compatibility of the raising standards and school inclusion agendas. Some key themes relating to these issues are summarised below.

The history and development of IEPs

Individualised Educational Programmes for children with SEN have developed in many parts of the industrialised world since the 1970s and reflect a range of influences and underlying philosophies of learning. In the 1970s and 1980s, behavioural psychologists occupied a powerful position within the field of special needs education (e.g. Brennan, 1974; Ainscow and Tweddle, 1979). They maintained that if a complex task could be analysed and broken into constituent parts, then each part could be taught until the child was able to undertake the entire activity. The component parts of each task were to be recorded within an IEP. This would be used by the teacher or instructor to record pupil progress and identify which steps should next be undertaken. The approach was popular because it appeared to offer a scientific basis to underpin the teaching on offer to a group of children seen as difficult to educate. However, it was also criticised as overly mechanistic and reductionist.

A second influence in the development of IEPs was the quest for an appropriate curriculum for children with SEN. As noted in Chapter 1, in Scotland children with complex needs have only been entitled to education since the mid-1970s and such children have never been easily accommodated within the mainstream curriculum. The introduction of the National Curriculum in England and the 5–14 programme in Scotland intensified debate about appropriate curriculum and pedagogy for children with high support needs. IEPs fitted well with a curriculum geared toward the achievement of developmental goals. Qualitative targets geared towards the individual needs of the child could be identified and modified at the teacher's discretion. Within this formulation, the IEP was an essentially open-ended document with the emphasis on charting the pupil's progress, but with little focus on measuring or comparing attainments against standardised benchmarks.

Finally, in the US the Individual Educational Plan has fulfilled a dual role, recording learning goals for the individual child, but also recording additional state/federal resources to be provided. The US Individual Educational Plan has the status of a legal document, with possible penalties for school districts and states if the provision specified is not delivered. Qualification for an Individual Educational Plan is based on tightly specified criteria, and disputes occur over boundaries and categories. In the US, about 12 per cent of school children have an Individual Educational Plan and a disproportionately high proportion of such children are black. From an equal opportunities perspective, attempts have been made to track the progress of children with Individual Educational Plans and measure the relative effectiveness of different schools. It has been suggested that legal contracts should be established 'with parents as equal participants in the plan, using objective measures of goal attainments, and developing punitive consequences for failure to deliver' (Goodman and Bond, 1993, p. 411). The legal sanctions for failure to achieve objectives was necessary because 'bureaucracies such as educational systems will move institutionally only under threat or duress' (Gallagher, 1972, p. 531).

To summarise, Individual Educational Plans are documents which encapsulate different views of how children learn and what accountability regimes are appropriate. In terms of systematic instruction and the developmental curriculum, teaching has to be geared towards the pupil's individual learning style and goals. It is appropriate for the teacher to record teaching objectives and pupil progress, but there is no expectation that outcomes can be aggregated and used to compare the overall effectiveness of particular schools for individual or groups of children. In contrast, some commentators in the US have suggested that teaching of children with SEN should be assessed using hard outcome measures and these should be used to make judgements about the effectiveness of particular schools, units and teachers. Despite these clear statements of principle, there appears to be little evidence of Individual Educational Plans in the US being used for this purpose. There are a number of reasons for this, but the fundamental problem is that assessing whether a child has attained a target involves a subjective judgement. Unless great efforts are made to validate the target and the evidence for its achievement, data will always be unreliable. In addition, each child with SEN is likely to have a unique profile so that it is very difficult to compare the attainments of individuals or groups.

The purpose of IEPs

Scottish IEPs are somewhat hybrid documents. The Scottish Executive's desire to make these targets measurable and to aggregate outcomes did not appear to sit easily with their original use by special needs teachers to record individual pupils' learning goals. Different perceptions of the purpose of IEPs were very apparent among key actors whose views were tapped within different elements of the research. Scottish Executive, teachers and local authority respondents emphasised the role of IEPs in recording individual learning goals and encouraging best practice by focusing the energies of practitioners on specified objectives. Whilst teachers and local authority respondents were critical of the idea that IEP targets could be used to make comparisons of the quality of SEN provision in different settings, a Scottish Executive respondent confirmed that this was a very important part of the initiative. He pointed out that schools with pupils with SEN 'cannot simply be left to set their own standards and select other schools with which to compare themselves'. An inspector suggested that comparisons between special schools were important, but had to be done on a voluntary basis. Schools had been encouraged to forge links with each other and compare the nature of targets set for particular children and outcomes achieved. However, any attempt to make this mandatory would be 'howled at by the teaching profession'.

Issues in setting and reviewing SMART targets

There was consensus from a wide range of respondents that the setting of SMART targets was very difficult in relation to many children with SEN.

Among our case studies, a senior teacher of children with social, emotional and behavioural difficulties spoke of the intermittent progress made by children, which did not reflect poor teaching, but rather a chaotic home life and erratic school attendance:

> We have many cases of children who achieve to the levels that have been set and beyond and overnight they have regressed away back because of a crisis at home. That's the difficulty for many of our children, it's the baggage they bring from home, the abuse, the neglect and the inappropriate parenting that impinges on their achievement.

Another head teacher commented on the difficulty of setting targets for children with degenerative conditions:

> I have no idea how somebody does that [target setting] for a child say with a degenerative disease, you know. When so much can hinge on the physical and mental well being. It must be heart-breaking and you send parents the copies of these [IEPs]. How do you make targets for somebody that's so ill? (Head teacher, special unit)

There was also a perception that it was difficult to judge whether developmental and aesthetic targets had been achieved. As a result, there was a possibility that teachers would focus their attention on goals that could be measured relatively easily, and other learning objectives which were less easy to measure might be neglected. A mainstream secondary head teacher included the following comment on the questionnaire:

> It is worrying that so much administration time will be put into managing the statistics of target-setting without necessarily increasing attainment . . . It may be that raising attainment in measurable areas is at the expense of attainments in other, equally important aspects of the curriculum.

Aggregating outcomes

As noted earlier, the use of IEPs was generally seen in positive terms. However, there was considerable hostility to the idea that there was any benefit at all in quantifying targets achieved and reporting school results to the Scottish Executive. A head teacher of a special school commented:

> I am absolutely convinced that we are going down the right track but I think it's fudged the benefits by throwing in all these percentages.

The likelihood of 'gaming' was noted, that is, the setting of targets which were easily achievable so that it could be reported that all targets had been met. A head teacher of a mainstream secondary commented:

> I think a lot of cheating will go on, I think that will basically be it. Schools will manufacture long-term targets which they know will be achievable so they look good. I think that's it in a nutshell. I don't think any school or learning centre is particularly going to go out on a wing. They're gonna play it safe.

It was evident that neither the Scottish Executive nor local authorities had any plans to moderate targets and were relying on schools to develop their internal moderating processes. Scottish Executive respondents reported that they were uncertain as to how to develop this initiative and it was possible that in the future the requirement to report outcomes would be dropped.

Involvement of key actors in the production of IEPs

The Scottish Executive hoped that, by linking the setting of targets to the production of IEPs, it would be possible to involve both parents and pupils closely in the process. Survey results suggested that in between a half and a third of schools, parents are not normally involved in the formulation and review of IEPs. Pupil involvement was particularly low in primary schools, with only 20 per cent of schools reporting that children were routinely involved in producing and reviewing IEPs.

With regard to professional involvement, there was strong evidence that IEPs were internal school documents in which other professionals had little involvement. Class or subject teachers and learning support staff were almost always involved, whereas educational psychologists were always involved in less than a quarter of all school and special units. Health professionals were involved in the production and review of IEPs in less than 50 per cent of schools overall and were less likely to be involved in mainstream than special schools and units. Overall, the Scottish Executive's ambition that the production and reviewing of targets would be an inclusive process involving family members and a wide range of professionals appeared not to have been achieved. The documents themselves and the learning goals remained the property of the school, with many parents expressing confusion about their purpose. For example, one parent commented:

> When I was presented [with the IEP], I hadn't a clue what SMART meant and I still don't really know what it means. To me, it's just paperwork.

Target setting and inclusion

As was noted at the start of this chapter, the Scottish Executive hoped that the raising attainment and the school inclusion agendas could sit happily alongside each other and be mutually reinforcing. There was evidence that, in some ways, IEPs with targets might magnify rather than diminish the separation of children with SEN from their peers. First, it was evident that most children with IEPs also had records of needs, so that IEPs were not being used to accommodate a wider group of children who might have some additional learning needs. A significantly higher proportion of pupils in mainstream primary (4 per cent) than secondary (2 per cent) had IEPs, and there was wide regional variation. Twenty per cent of pupils in special secondary schools did not have an IEP.

In mainstream secondary schools, it was observed by local authority and school staff that it was very difficult to involve subject staff in setting and reviewing targets and incorporating an awareness of individual pupils' targets into classroom teaching. Children with IEPs were seen as the responsibility of learning support staff. A local authority respondent expressed the fear that, in the future, group IEPs might be produced for secondary school pupils with learning difficulties and they might be taught a restricted curriculum in a 'remedial' class. If this were to happen, it would clearly be at odds with inclusive principles.

Finally, as noted earlier, there was considerable anxiety about the impact of reporting the performance of children with SEN alongside the performance of other children in the school. Since many parents tended to judge schools on their raw results, including children with SEN in the reporting of targets might have a negative impact on the public perception of the school. In the interests of inclusion, the Scottish Executive insisted that children with SEN should be included in mainstream reporting of outcomes, as well as in relation to performance on targets specified within the IEP. Clearly, for schools and the Scottish Executive, there are difficulties in reconciling the desire to value all children in terms of their individual achievements, and the recognition that socially exclusive institutions are likely to be judged as 'better' schools and selected by middle-class parents.

Conclusion

Scotland has traditionally placed a great deal of importance on school self-regulation and this has been particularly marked in the sphere of SEN. Until recently, children with SEN could be excused from national assessments and progress was tracked on an individual basis by the child's teacher, with no external moderating or reporting. The Scottish Executive's initiative on raising the attainment of pupils with SEN tried to introduce much higher levels of accountability into special needs education in the spirit of inclusiveness. Evidence suggests that the initiative has had mixed success. Whilst teachers approved of setting learning objectives for children with SEN as a means of improving teaching and learning, they were sceptical about whether it was feasible or desirable to aggregate such data and use it as the basis for making judgements about the effectiveness of teachers or schools. Using Power's (1997) terminology, there were fears of 'colonisation', implying that teachers might focus on those areas of the curriculum which could be readily measured and neglect 'soft' learning outcomes. Alternatively, it was suggested that in mainstream secondary schools a process of 'decoupling' might take place, so that pupils with learning difficulties might receive a restricted curriculum in a segregated setting delivered by learning support staff. It was evident that developing and reviewing targets within IEPs was seen as the preserve of school staff. Parents, pupils and other professionals were often marginalised in this process. Finally, reporting the learning attainments of children among mainstream school statistics was seen as potentially anti-inclusive, in that elite schools would find ways of discouraging children with SEN so that their position at the top of league tables would be protected. In the light of these difficulties, it appeared that there was a retreat from earlier plans to enforce strict accountability regimes in relation to pupils with SEN. Two years after the implementation of the target-setting initiative, the requirement to report aggregated targets was dropped.

With the implementation of the new additional support for learning legislation, IEPs will have an even higher status, since many children who would formerly have received a record of needs will, in the future, have an IEP rather than a CSP. This research revealed very different understanding of their content, purpose and format, and it may be necessary to ensure a greater degree of commonality to guard against inequities based on geographical location.

Chapter 6

DISABILITY RIGHTS AND INCLUSION

Introduction

In this concluding chapter, we first consider the implications of the extension of the Disability Discrimination Act 1995 (DDA) to education before reviewing some of the policy tensions within the field of special and additional supportneeds education which have been explored in earlier chapters. Within the industrialised world, there are different approaches to protecting the rights of disabled people. The US introduced anti-discrimination legislation for disabled people in 1990. The Americans with Disabilities Act 1990 (ADA) provided equal opportunity and access for people with disabilities, prohibiting discrimination on the basis of disability in employment, state and local government, public accommodations, commercial facilities, transportation and telecommunications. The Individuals with Disabilities Act 1990 (IDEA) related more specifically to education and, amongst other things, required schools to prepare children for adult life. Most European countries have not introduced anti-discrimination legislation, protecting the rights of disabled people by measures such as quota systems, which require organisations to include a certain percentage of disabled people within the workforce and fining them for failure to comply. Great Britain is closer to countries such as the US and Australia, abandoning its employment quota system and introducing anti discrimination measures in the mid-1990s.

The Conservative government was unenthusiastic about the introduction of the legislation and blocked it many times before it finally reached the statute book. Initially, the DDA applied only to the fields of employment, services and the sale or rental of property. The prohibition on employment discrimination only applied to employers with more than 15 employees in total and did not apply to members of the armed forces; prison officers; barristers; fire-fighters; employees who work wholly or mainly outside Great Britain; employees on board ships, aircraft or hovercraft; police officers. The prohibition on discrimination in the provision of goods and services did not apply to education or transport services. Furthermore, the impact of the DDA on government was restricted by Section 53 of the Act, which stated that anything which is done 'in pursuance of an act of parliament will be lawful even if it would otherwise amount to discrimination'.

The exclusion of education from the DDA was a source of great disappointment to the disability movement, since education is central to the future life chances of children and young people. The incoming New Labour government in 1997 set up a Disability Rights Task Force which, in its report *From Exclusion to Inclusion* (DfEE, 1999) came up with 150 recommendations for the extension of the DDA. The government's response to the DRTF report (DfEE, 2001) set out its plans for the extension of the DDA. These included repealing the small employer threshold, increasing the duties of providers of goods and services and extending the legislation to cover education. The Special Educational Needs and Disability Act 2001, Part 4 of the DDA, came into effect in England, Wales and Scotland in September 2002. Two separate Codes of Practice were published by the Disability Rights Commission to explain the legislation, one dealing with schools (DRC, 2002b) and one dealing with post-16 provision (2002a).

Whilst there has been some criticism of the legislation on the grounds that it uses a normative rather than a social model definition of disability and is still limited in its scope, nonetheless it is seen as very important in terms of giving political recognition to disabled people. The creation of the Disability Rights Commission in 2000 was also seen as important both practically and symbolically, signifying the government's commitment to enforce the legislation. Gooding (2000), assessing the impact of the Act, suggests that it marks 'a huge leap forward in society's understanding of disability' and in 'disabled people's image of themselves'.

This chapter provides a brief summary of the legislation as it applies to schools and considers its future impact on justice in the field of SEN. Finally, it reviews some of the policy tensions which have been identified in the course of this book and considers how they may be resolved in the future.

The Special Educational Needs and Disability Act 2001: territorial coverage

Under the terms of the Scotland Act 1998, responsibility for equal opportunities is reserved to Westminster, although responsibility for the implementation of equal opportunities policies is devolved to the Scottish Parliament. Whilst Part 4 of the DDA applies throughout Great Britain (Northern Ireland has separate equality legislation), it is implemented through the separate educational frameworks of Scotland, England and Wales. Those drafting the statutory codes to accompany the legislation faced an interesting challenge in ensuring that the anti-discrimination principles of the DDA should be applied equally within the different SEN frameworks. As noted earlier, the English SEN policy framework was informed by versions of procedural justice rooted in legality, managerialism, marketisation and consumerism compared with the Scottish system, which was still heavily influenced by the traditional models of bureaucracy and professionalism, albeit overlaid by these other policy frameworks. As the provisions of Part 4 of the DDA are put into practice, it is likely that the Scottish system will be forced to take greater account of the rights of parents and children, and it is interesting that the impetus for this shift in focus should have come from Westminster rather than Scottish legislation.

Provisions of Part 4 of the DDA

The legislation places two key duties on education providers (referred to in the Act as 'responsible bodies'). These are:

- not to treat disabled pupils/prospective pupils less favourably; and
- to make reasonable adjustments to avoid putting disabled pupils at a substantial disadvantage.

The second duty is limited in the following ways:

- Reasonable adjustment duties do not require the responsible body to provide auxiliary aids and services.
- Reasonable adjustment duties do not require the responsible body to make alterations to the physical features of the school.

It was assumed that these areas were covered by the existing SEN framework and this point is considered further below. The type of reasonable adjustments that are required by the Act include ensuring that teaching and assessment materials are accessible to all pupils, for example, are available in large font for pupils with visual impairments or in simplified format for pupils with learning difficulties. In addition, schools will be expected to ensure that classes are in locations which are accessible. This may simply require an alteration in room allocation, so that a class attended by a disabled child takes place in an accessible ground floor location.

The duty not to treat disabled pupils less favourably for a reason relating to their disability without justification also has important implications. It means that a disabled pupil may not be discriminated against in admissions, exclusions, or in the provision of any education-related service. There are some circumstances where it may be lawful to treat a disabled pupil less favourably for a reason relating to his or her disability. For instance, if the presence of a disabled child might have a detrimental effect on the education of other children, for example, by behaving in a very disruptive or violent fashion, then the school might be justified in educating the child elsewhere. However, the local authority would need to be able to demonstrate that it had taken all reasonable steps to include the child. These might include training staff, offering appropriate support to the pupil, making adjustments to the curriculum and so on. If the local authority had not taken these steps, then it might be found to have acted unlawfully.

It is important to note that schools in the independent sector as well as the state sector are covered by the Act. Some schools in the independent sector may have traditionally paid little attention to ensuring disability equality because the existing SEN framework only applies to local authority provision. However, from September 2002, like state schools, they have been prohibited from discriminating against disabled pupils or prospective pupils in any of their admissions, teaching or assessment policies and practices. Less favourable treatment of disabled children for a reason relating to their disability may be justified if it is the result of a permitted form of selection, or if there is a reason which is material to the circumstances of the particular case, and is substantial. It is clear that the selection and exclusion practices of independent schools may be open to legal challenge.

The DDA's definition of disability

Under the DDA, a disabled person is defined as someone who has a physical or mental disability which has an effect on his or her ability to carry out normal day-to-day activities. That effect must be:

- substantial (that is more then minor or trivial); and
- adverse; and
- long-term (that is, has lasted or is likely to last for at least a year or for the rest of the life of the person affected).

Physical disability was not defined, but at least initially mental disability is defined to include learning disabilities and mental health problems if these were 'clinically well recognised conditions'. This definition raises questions about whether more parents will seek to have their children diagnosed with a specific condition, such as Attention Deficit and Hyper-Active Disorder (ADHD) in order to gain protection under the Act. Some conditions are explicitly excluded from the Act. These include drug or alcohol addiction or dependency; hay fever; tendency to set fires; tendency to steal; tendency to physical or sexual abuse of other persons; exhibitionism; and voyeurism. Normal day-to-day activities include mobility; manual dexterity; physical co-ordination; continence; ability to lift, carry or otherwise move everyday objects; speech, hearing or eyesight; memory or ability to concentrate, learn or understand; and perception of the risk of physical dangers. It is worth noting that establishing disability is a major hurdle for applicants under the DDA. By way of contrast, those seeking protection under race and sex discrimination legislation do not have to undergo a similar test.

The definition of disability within the DDA is different from the definition of additional support needs in the Education (Additional Support for Learning) (Scotland) Act 2004. As noted earlier, a child or young person is said to have additional support needs if he or she for whatever reason, 'is likely to be unable to benefit from school education provided or to be provided for the child or young person'. In terms of its circularity, this definition resembles the definition of learning difficulty in the Education (Scotland) Act 1980, which states that a child or young person has a learning difficulty if he or she:

a) has a significantly greater difficulty in learning than the majority of those of his or her age; or

b) has a disability which either prevents or hinders him or her from making effective use of educational facilities of a kind generally provided in schools managed by his local authority; or

c) is under the age of 5 years and is, or would be if special provision was not made for him or her, be likely, when over that age, to have a learning difficulty as defined above.

Definitions of children in need within the Children (Scotland) Act 1995, which include disabled children and children adversely affected by disability, also differ from education and DDA definitions. Children and young people classified as disabled under the DDA definition would clearly be a sub-set of the much larger group encompassed in these other legal definitions. It is likely that some children who are covered by the DDA will not be identified as having additional support needs. For example, a child with a physical disability who can cope perfectly well with the 5–14 Curriculum may not be defined as having a learning difficulty and may not have a co-ordinated Support Plan or an IEP, but nonetheless may be covered by the DDA. Similarly, a child who has been identified at school as having a specific learning difficulty, for instance, a child with a mild form of dyslexia, may not be covered by the DDA.

Knowing which pupils are disabled

Under the DDA, it is up to a court to decide whether someone is disabled or not. However, responsible bodies (local authorities and schools) have to ensure that they have taken all reasonable actions to identify which children are disabled and who therefore may require reasonable adjustments. In order to be proactive in identifying which children are disabled, schools must ensure that there is an open and welcoming atmosphere, ask parents when they visit the school whether their child has a disability and have a space on admissions forms requesting this information. If a parent has informed a school employee about a child's disability, then the school is deemed to have been informed. For example, if a school secretary has been informed that a child has diabetes, it is assumed that this information will be conveyed to all other staff in the school who need this information. If a parent or a pupil asks a school to keep confidential the fact that a pupil has a disability, or the nature of that disability, the responsible body must comply with this request. Clearly, schools and local authorities will have to review their policies on identifying disabled pupils and communicating information about them to school employees.

Relationship of the DDA to the existing additional support needs framework

Guidance on the new duties suggests that it is helpful to think of the legislation in terms of a jigsaw of provision, so that the new measures dovetail with existing legislation. The Education (Additional Support for Learning) (Scotland) Act 1980 places duties on local authorities to identify and meet the needs of children requiring extra help to benefit from education. Ultimately, as the responsible body for education, the local authority has a duty to ensure that the necessary services and resources are in place. However, local authorities are increasingly delegating budgets to schools, and assuming they are using these funds to provide the necessary support to individual children, such as a behaviour support assistant. As noted earlier, under the DDA, the reasonable adjustments which responsible bodies are expected to make do not include the provision of auxiliary aids and services nor adjustments to physical features. When the disability legislation was being drafted, it was assumed that such provision would be made under the existing education framework, and it was felt that making provision under two different strands of legislation would cause confusion. However, CSPs which are likely to specify resources will only be held by a very small proportion of children, and IEPs do not always stipulate what additional resources will be provided. Additionally, some children with additional support needs may not have an IEP. In the future, it may be very difficult to hold local authorities to account if they are failing to provide sufficient resources to support children with significant difficulties but who lack the protection of a CSP. Unlike England and Wales, at the time of writing, disability discrimination cases are not heard by the Additional Support Needs Tribunal, but redress has to be sought through the more tortuous route of the Sheriff Court.

Planning duties

Since planning matters are devolved to the Scottish Parliament, the planning duties within the Special Educational Needs and Disability Act 2001 do not apply to Scotland. However, as flagged up in Chapter 1, The Education (Disability Strategies and Pupils' Educational Records) (Scotland) Act, implemented from September 2002, places a duty on responsible bodies to publish and implement accessibility strategies for the school(s) for which they have responsibility. Accessibility is defined broadly, so that it covers the physical environment, the curriculum and communication methods. From September 2002, local authorities and schools are expected to anticipate and plan for the needs of disabled pupils before they arrive at a school, rather than putting in place emergency measures when a pupil with a particular impairment arrives. Whilst many local authorities may have been unaware of their new duties under the DDA, they will be unable to ignore the new planning requirements and these are likely to have a positive impact on approaches to the inclusion of disabled pupils in mainstream education. An evaluation of the first set of plans (Scottish Executive, 2003), however, showed that many authorities tended to focus on the physical environment, and much less progress had been made in planning for access to school information, the curriculum and assessment. Independent schools' plans were very weak, and suggested a limited understanding of the legislation, with a tendency to favour strategies which might avoid legal action but did little to promote the spirit of the Act. Making the curriculum far more accessible is clearly an area which needs to be addressed by the *Curriculum for Excellence* programme.

Redress and conciliation

Under the DDA, if a parent or child believes that discrimination has occurred, then they are encouraged to complain to the school and/or the local authority so that, if at all possible, the problem can be ironed out at an early stage. They may also contact the Disability Rights Commission for help and advice. Finally, if the matter cannot be resolved through conciliation, a case may be brought to the Sheriff Court. The Disability Rights Commission hopes to bring a number of test cases to establish legal precedents.

In England, parents have for some time had stronger rights of redress, since they have been able to bring cases to the Special Educational Needs Tribunal established under the terms of the Education Act 1993. Under the Special Educational Needs and Disability Act 2001, the SENT was renamed the Special Educational Needs and Disability Tribunal (SENDIST) and its remit extended so that it would hear all cases relating to SEN and disability discrimination. The Scottish system, which involved education appeals being made to Scottish Ministers or to Education Appeal Committees, and disability discrimination cases being referred to the Sheriff Court, appeared to be cumbersome, time-consuming and very unfriendly for users. However, the establishment or extension of local authority mediation services and a tribunal system (Scottish Executive, 2002) may offer a more accessible approach to legal redress, according greater rights to children and parents. At the time of writing, however, it appears that, because of the very strict criteria for making a reference, and the exclusion of disability discrimination cases, very few references are being made to the Additional Support Needs Tribunal in Scotland compared with the Tribunals in England and Wales.

The future significance of disability discrimination legislation

In order for the DDA to be effective in challenging discriminatory practices in education, considerable effort will have to be invested in ensuring that it is implemented according to the spirit of the law and that minimal compliance is avoided. Regular monitoring will play an important part here, but, in addition, continuing pressure on government from disabled people and their supporters will be required. Gooding (1994) noted that 'For an anti-discrimination law to have any real capacity to achieve its goals it must be the product and instrument of a powerful collective movement' (p. 173). Anti-discrimination legislation cannot by itself dismantle structural disadvantage, but is an essential element in such change. The DDA has the capacity to widen the models of procedural justice within the Scottish SEN system, pushing the balance of power towards children and parents. However, there is evidence of resistance to any democratisation of power in the field of additional support needs. For example, the Association of Principal Educational Psychologists declared their opposition to the establishment of mediation and tribunal systems during the consultation phase, seeing these as possibly creating an overly adversarial system. The way in which these struggles play out between actors with competing agendas will provide fascinating terrain for future research.

We have already discussed the implications of recent disability discrimination legislation in establishing new models of procedural justice within the field of additional support needs. These will involve new positive and negative trade-offs. For instance, socially advantaged individuals who can purchase the services of knowledgeable lawyers are likely to have more success in claiming their rights than individuals who lack such resources. Less attention may be paid to issues of collective justice when the emphasis is on individuals claiming their rights.

Categorisation versus rejection of labelling

This book has traced ongoing tensions between those who argue for the utility of categorising and identifying disabled children and those who maintain that such attempts should always be regarded with extreme suspicion. During the twentieth century, statutory categories of handicap were introduced, but were subsequently seen as stigmatising and were replaced by the unitary category of 'special educational needs'. The DDA introduced new categories of disability based on a normative assessment of a child's mental and physical functioning rather than their educational requirements. It is inevitable that, as the new duties placed on responsible bodies are applied, tensions will arise between the different definitions of disability in education, social work and disability discrimination legislation, since each implies a different approach to assessment and identification. The definition of disability in the DDA has been challenged by social modellists, who argue that the emphasis should be on identifying the social adjustments which are required rather than individual deficits. However, operationalising a social model definition of disability within a legal structure appears to be technically challenging. There are interesting international comparisons to be made here. Whilst some, but not all, European countries have moved away from categorical systems, the US continues to work with strict qualification criteria for Individual Educational Plans, since these are high-stakes, legally-enforceable documents which are able to attract resourcing targeted at the individual child (Florian *et al.*, 2006)

Disability: a privileged or stigmatised category?

At the root of debates over the justification for the use of categories of disability lies an uncertainty as to whether disability may be seen as a positive or negative status. The disability movement has argued strongly that it is important to see being disabled as a positive political and cultural identity, but some writers acknowledge that it is easier to feel positive about some types of impairment rather than others. For example, whilst the life of a child injured in a land mine explosion must be celebrated and enhanced, it is impossible to feel positive about the fact that this injury occurred in the first place. Such debates quickly lead into current controversies over pre-natal screening and selective abortion, where some argue that the overriding factor has to be a woman's right to decide whether to go ahead with a pregnancy, whilst others argue that the right to life is of paramount importance and that permitting the abortion of a disabled foetus (where the normal time limits for abortion do not apply) implies that less value is placed on the life of a disabled person. Such debates are complicated by divisions within the disability movement, with some deaf people, for example, rejecting the identity of disability and instead claiming the status of a linguistic minority.

The DDA and other social security legislation are based on the assumption that being disabled accords certain rights and privileges, such as financial support and the requirement that service providers will make reasonable adjustments to accommodate needs. However, it is unclear that the positive aspects of being identified as disabled outweigh the negative effects of stigmatisation and marginalisation. Writers like Tomlinson (1982) have warned that, whilst categorisation may appear benign, it may often have hidden malign effects and McDonnell (2000) draws on the writings of Foucault to suggest that within SEN attempts to categorise are likely to be accompanied by a range of disciplinary mechanisms which restrict, rather than enhance, the experience of individuals.

One way to resolve the tension between categorisation and anti-labelling approaches may be to recognise the importance of who is categorising and for what purpose. Nonetheless, systems which are initially informed by good intentions, such as the suggestion that a register should be maintained of people with learning disabilities to permit the planning of appropriate services, may subsequently be used by those with less benign intentions.

It is interesting to note that, whenever efforts are made to remove categories, they appear to creep back in different forms. For example, Warnock's anti-labelling approach was followed by the emergence of 'new' disabilities such as dyspraxia, autism and ADHD.

Inclusive versus specialist provision

It is evident that the thrust of both official policy documents and legislation is currently toward including as many disabled children as possible in mainstream schools. However, some unresolved policy tensions remain in this area also. Whilst some parents feel that local authorities drag their heels in relation to inclusion, others are in dispute with local authorities because of their refusal to fund specialist educational provision for their children. Some parents of children with autistic spectrum disorder, for instance, feel that mainstream or even generic special schools are unable to meet their child's needs, and seek placement in specialist independent schools. Parents are also keen to retain specialist qualifications for teachers of children with specific impairments, maintaining that generic qualifications or deregulation fail to provide teachers with the detailed knowledge of particular impairments and appropriate instruction techniques. New forms of segregation are also likely to emerge. For example, as noted in Chapter 4, the closure of special schools has been accompanied by the rapid increase in the number of special units attached to mainstream. A child in such a unit may have his or her name on a mainstream roll, but spend little time in inclusive settings. Whilst there is now a presumption of mainstream placement, the Scottish Executive endorses the continued existence of special schools and acknowledges the right of parents and children to request such placements. In the future, it will be important to continue to monitor the status and use of the special sector. We also noted that children are spatially excluded from school in many ways other than through special school placement, including formal exclusion from school. The operation of all forms of formal and informal spatial exclusion requires further investigation.

Raising standards versus achieving inclusion

Scottish and UK administrations are committed to the dual policies of raising standards and increasing social inclusion. It is argued that such policies should be compatible and Chapter 5 reported on an initiative geared towards including children with additional support needs in accountability initiatives geared towards improving learning and teaching. The research reported in Chapter 5 revealed some tensions between the policies. Setting SMART targets within IEPs was seen as a good way of sharpening teachers' approach to the education of children with additional support needs by focusing attention on teaching objectives and children's progress. However, attempts to aggregate outcomes with a view to assessing the relative effectiveness of different schools and sectors was rejected by local authorities and teachers on the grounds that this would encourage the setting of easily achieved targets and the over-claiming of positive outcomes. Including children with additional support needs in the reporting of examination and test results was seen as promoting a tendency to exclude such children, particularly in schools wishing to maintain their position at the top of the league tables. The following unresolved paradox appears to remain in this area: if children with additional support needs are excluded from accountability regimes, this may signal that their progress is less important than that of other children. On the other hand, their inclusion may produce unwanted exclusionary pressures within mainstream schools. This problem requires greater attention in the future.

Building human capital and promoting social justice

Many debates in the area of SEN are informed by underlying, but often unspoken, concerns about how much money should be spent on the education of children with additional support needs compared with others. From a human capital perspective, which often dominates educational discourse, it may be argued that children with additional support needs may be expensive to educate but yield relatively little in terms of contributing to future national economic competitiveness. On the other hand, human capitalists have argued that some investment is necessary in the education of children at risk of social exclusion to ensure that they are able to make a modest living rather than being a 'burden on the state' (for a somewhat stark expression of this view, see the discussions of the Egerton Committee, reported in Chapter 1). From a social justice perspective, expenditure on education should not be calculated in relation to an individual's future profitability, but that individual's needs. Whilst local authorities claim to operate needs-led budgets in educating children with additional support needs, Directors of Education frequently complain of budgetary overspends in this area. Whilst it would be wrong to claim that the review of assessment and recording has been driven by financial concerns, it would be disingenuous to argue that financial concerns were irrelevant, particularly in local authority responses to the consultation. It appears that local authorities do not like committing funds to individual children. On the other hand, if some children are deprived of the type of individual support they require, mainstream placement is unlikely to work effectively and the backlash against inclusion will be fuelled.

Conclusion

To return to the starting-point of this book, the field of additional support needs provides important insights into tensions within the education system not just for children requiring special support, but also for their non-disabled peers. This concluding chapter has attempted to pull together the key questions which have threaded their way through the text. What version of procedural justice should pre-dominate in the management of special needs education and whose interests should be prioritised? What are the pros and cons of categorising children with SEN? Is a disabled identity something to be embraced or denied? Is there any place in future education systems for separate provision for some groups of disabled children? If so, what form should it take and who should it be designed for? Is it possible to devise accountability systems which include disabled children without creating perverse incentives for their exclusion? What proportion of the education budget should be spent on children with additional support needs relative to others? There are, of course, no easy answers to any of these questions. Solutions emerging at any particular time will involve different sets of positive and negative trade-offs. However, it is very clear that decisions about education in general, and about special needs education, will have consequences for the system as a whole. It is hoped that an understanding of this iterative relationship will inform future debates on education, and that the field of additional support needs is not treated as a separate cul de sac.

REFERENCES

Accounts Commission for Scotland (2002) *Comparing the Performance of Scottish Councils: Education 2000/01*, Edinburgh: Accounts Commission for Scotland

Adler, M. (1997) 'Looking backwards to the future: Parental choice and education Policy', *British Educational Research Journal*, Vol. 23, No. 3, pp. 297–315

Adler, M. (2001) 'Substantive justice and procedural fairness in social security', in Kjonstad, A. (ed.) (2001) *Law and Poverty*, Oxford: Hart Publishing

Adler, M. and Sainsbury, R. (1991) 'Administrative justice, quality of service and the operational strategy', in Adler, M. and Williams, R. (eds) *Social Implications of the Operational Strategy*, New Waverley Papers – Social Policy Series No. 4, Edinburgh: Department of Social Policy, University of Edinburgh

Ainscow, M. and Tweddle, D. A. (1979) *Preventing Classroom Failure: An Objectives Approach*, London: Wiley

Allan, J., Brown, S. and Munn, P. (1991) *Off the Record: Mainstream Provision for Pupils with Non-Recorded Difficulties in Mainstream Primary and Secondary Schools*, Edinburgh: Scottish Council for Research in Education

Armstrong, A., Belmont, B. and Verillon, A. (2000a) ' "Vive la difference?" Exploring content, policy and change in special education in France: developing cross-cultural collaboration', in Armstrong *et al.* (eds) (2000b), pp. 60–78

Armstrong, F., Armstrong, D. and Barton, L. (eds) (2000b) *Inclusive Education: Policy, Contexts and Comparative Perspectives*, London: David Fulton Publishers

Audit Commission (2002) *Statutory Assessment and Statements of SEN: In Need of Review?* London: Audit Commission

Banks, P., Baynes, A., Dyson, A., Kane, J., Millward, A., Riddell, S. and Wilson, A. (2001) *Raising the Attainment of Pupils with Special Educational Needs*, Report to the Scottish Executive Education Department, Glasgow: Strathclyde Centre for Disability Research, University of Glasgow

Barnes, C. (1991) *Disabled People in Britain and Discrimination: A Case for Anti-Discrimination Legislation*, London: Hurst & Co.

Booth, T. (2000) 'Inclusion and exclusion policy in England: who controls the agenda?', in Armstrong *et al.* (eds) (2000), pp. 78–99

Borland, M., Pearson, C. C., Hill, M., Tisdall, K. and Bloomfield, I. (1998) *The Education of Children Looked After Away from Home*, Edinburgh, Scottish Council for Research in Education

Bowers, T. and Wilkinson, D. (1998) 'The SEN Code of Practice: is it user-friendly?' *British Journal of Special Education*, Vol. 25, No. 3, pp. 19–125

Brennan, W. K. (1974) *Shaping the Education of Slow Learners*, London: Routledge and Kegan Paul

The Cabinet Office (1999) *Modernising Government*, London: Cabinet Office

Clarke, J. and Newman, J. (1997) *The Managerial State*, London: Sage.

Corbett, J. and Slee, R. (2000) 'An international conversation on inclusive education', in Armstrong *et al.* (eds) (2000b), pp. 133–47

Corker, M. (1998) 'Disability discourse in a post-modern world', in Shakespeare, T. (ed.) (1998) *The Disability Reader*, London: Cassell, pp. 221–34

Deakin, N. (1994) *The Politics of Welfare: Continuities and Change*, London: Harvester Wheatsheaf

Department of Constitutional Affairs (2004) *Transforming Public Services: Complaints, Redress and Tribunals*, London: The Stationery Office

Department for Education (1994a) *Code of Practice on the Identification and Assessment of Special Educational Needs*, London: DfE

Department for Education (1994b) *Special Educational Needs: A Guide for Parents*, London: DfEE

Department for Education and Employment (1997) *Excellence for All Children: Meeting Special Educational Needs*, London: DfEE

Department for Education and Employment (1999) *From Exclusion to Inclusion; A Report of the Disability Rights Task Force*, London: DfEE

Department for Education and Employment (2001) *Towards Inclusion – Civil Rights for Disabled People; Government response to the Disability Rights Task Force*, London: DfEE

Department for Education and Science (1978) *Special Educational Needs* (The Warnock Report), London: HMSO

Department for Education and Skills (2001) *SEN Code of Practice on the Identification and Assessment of Pupils with Special Educational Needs*, London: DfES

Department for Education and Skills (2003) *Every Child Matters*, London: DfES

Department for Education and Skills (2004) *Removing Barriers to Achievement – The Government's Strategy for Special Educational Needs*, London: DfES

Disability Rights Commission (2002a) *Code of Practice Post-16: Code of Practice for Post-16 Providers of Education and Related Services*, London: The Stationery Office

Disability Rights Commission (2002b) *Code of Practice for Schools*, London: The Stationery Office

Educational Institute of Scotland (2006) *Supporting Teachers, Tackling Indiscipline*, Edinburgh: EIS

Evans, J. (1998) *Getting it Right: LEAs and the Special Educational Needs Tribunal*, Slough: National Foundation for Educational Research

Evans, J. (1999) 'The impact of the Special Educational Needs Tribunal on local educational authorities' policy and planning for special educational needs', *Support for Learning: British Journal of Learning Support*, Vol. 14, No. 2, pp. 74–80

Fairley, J. and Paterson, L. (1995) 'Scottish education and the new managerialism', *Scottish Educational Review*, Vol. 27, pp. 13–36

Fergusson, R. (2000) 'Modernizing managerialism in education', in Clarke, J., Gewirtz, S. and McLaughlin, E. (eds) (2000) *New Managerialism, New Welfare*, London: Sage

Florian, L., Hollenweger, J., Simeonsson, R., Weddell, K. J., Riddell, S., Terzi, L. and Holland, A. (2006) 'Cross-cultural perspectives on the classification of children with disabilities, Part 1: issues in the classification of children with disabilities', *The Journal of Special Education*, Vol. 40, No. 1, pp. 36–46

Florian, L. and Pullin, D. (2000) 'Defining difference: a comparative perspective on legal and policy issues in education reform and special educational needs', in McLaughlin, M. J. and Rouse, M. (eds) *Special Education and School Reform in the United States and Britain*, London: RoutledgeFalmer, pp. 11–38

Gallagher, J. (1975) 'The special education contract for mildly handicapped children', *Exceptional Children*, Vol. 38, pp. 527–35

Garner, P. (1996) '"Go forth and co-ordinate!" What special educational needs co-ordinators think about the Code of Practice', *School Organisation*, Vol. 16, No. 2, pp. 179–86

Gooding, C. (1994) *Disabling Laws, Enabling Acts*, London: Pluto Press

Gooding, C. (2000) 'Disability Discrimination Act: from statute to practice', *Critical Social Policy*, Vol. 20, No. 4, pp. 533–49

Goodman, J. F. and Bond, L. (1993) 'The Individualised Educational Programme: a retrospective critique', *The Journal of Special Education*, Vol. 26, No. 4, pp. 408–22

Hargreaves, D. (1990) 'Making schools more effective: the challenge to policy, practice and research', *Scottish Educational Review*, Vol. 22, No. 1, pp. 5–14

Harris, N. (1997) *Special Educational Needs and Access to Justice*, Bristol: Jordans

Hegarty, S. (1989) 'Special educational needs and national testing', *Support for Learning*, Vol. 4, No. 4, pp. 205–8

Heward, C. and Lloyd-Smith, M. (1990) 'Assessing the impact of legislation on special education policy – an historical analysis', *Journal of Education Policy*, Vol. 5, No. 1, pp. 21–36

Kane, J., Riddell, S., Banks, P., Baynes, A., Dyson, A., Millward, A. and Wilson, A. (2003) 'Special educational needs and individualised educational programmes: issues of parent and pupil participation', *Scottish Educational Review*, Vol. 35, No. 1, pp. 38–48

Kirp, D. (1982) 'Professionalisation as policy choice: British special education in comparative perspective', *World Politics*, Vol. XXXIV, No. 2, pp. 137–74

Lewis, A. and Norwich B. (2005) *Special Teaching for Special Children*? Buckingham: Open University Press

Lipsky, M. (1980) *Street-Level Bureaucracy*, New York: Russell Sage Foundation

McDonnell, P. (2000) 'Inclusive education in Ireland: rhetoric and reality', in Armstrong *et al.* (eds) (2000), pp. 12–27

McPherson, A. and Raab, C. (1988) *Governing Education: A Sociology of Policy Since 1945*, Edinburgh: Edinburgh University Press

Male, D. B. and May, D. (1997) 'Stress, burnout and workload in teachers of children with special educational needs', *British Journal of Special Education*, Vol. 24, No. 3, pp. 133–40

Mashaw, J. L. (1983) *Bureaucratic Justice: Managing Social Security Disability Claims*, New Haven and London: Yale University Press

Mason, M. (1993) *Inclusion: The Way Forward; A Guide to Integration for Young Disabled Children*, London: Voluntary Organisation Liaison Council for Under Fives

Mercer, N. (2001) 'Talking and working together', in Wearmouth (ed.) (2001), pp. 187–216

Merrett, F. (2001) 'Helping teachers who have fallen behind', in Wearmouth (ed.) (2001), pp. 216–28

Millward, A. and Skidmore, D. (1998) 'LEA responses to the management of special education in the light of the Code of Practice', *Educational Management and Administration*, Vol. 26, No. 1, pp. 57–66

Mooney, G. and Scott, G. (eds) (2006) *Exploring Social Policy in the 'New' Scotland*, Bristol: Policy Press

Munn, P., Johnstone, M. and Sharp, S. (2004) *Teachers' Perceptions of Discipline in Scottish Schools: Final Report to the Scottish Executive*, Edinburgh: University of Edinburgh

Newman, J. (2001) *Modernising Governance: New Labour, Policy and Society*, London: Sage

OECD (2005) *Students with Disabilities, Learning Difficulties and Disadvantages: Statistics and Indicators*, Paris: OECD/CERI

Pickles, P. (2001) 'Therapeutic provision in mainstream curricula for pupils with severe motor difficulties', in Wearmouth (ed.) (2001), pp. 291–305

Pinney, A. (2004) *Reducing Reliance on Statements: An Investigation into Local Authority Practice and Outcomes*, DFES Research Report 508, Nottingham: DfES

Pollitt, C. (1993) *Managerialism and the Public Services*, Oxford: Blackwell

Power, M. (1997) *The Audit Society*, Oxford: Oxford University Press

Riddell, S. (1997) 'Education', in Ffyfe, G. (ed.) *Why the Poor Pay More*, Glasgow: Scottish Consumer Council

Riddell, S., Adler, M., Farmakopoulou, N. and Mordaunt, E. (2000) 'Special educational needs and competing policy frameworks in England and Scotland', *Journal of Education Policy*, Vol. 15, No. 6, pp. 621–35

Riddell, S. and Brown, S. (eds) (1991) *School Effectiveness Research: Its Messages for School Improvement*, Edinburgh: HMSO

Riddell, S., Tinklin, T. and Wilson, A. (2005) *Disabled Students in Higher Education: Perspectives on Widening Access and Changing Policy*, London: RoutledgeFalmer

Riddell, S., Wilson, A., Adler, M. and Mordaunt, E. (2002) 'Parents, professionals and SEN policy frameworks in England and Scotland', *Policy and Politics*, Vol. 30, No. 3, pp. 411–27

Scottish Education Department (1978) *The Education of Pupils with Learning Difficulties in Primary and Secondary Schools in Scotland: A Progress Report by HM Inspector of Schools*, Edinburgh: HMSO

Scottish Executive (1999) *Improving our Schools: Consultation on the Improvement in Scottish Education Bill*, Edinburgh: Scottish Executive

Scottish Executive (2000a) *The Same as You? A Review of Services for People with Learning Disabilities*, Edinburgh: Scottish Executive

Scottish Executive (2000b) *Social Justice: A Scotland Where Everyone Matters: Annual Report 2000*, Edinburgh: Scottish Executive

Scottish Executive (2001a) *Better Behaviour – Better Learning: The Report of the Discipline Task Group*, Edinburgh: Scottish Executive

Scottish Executive (2001b) *For Scotland's Children: Better Integrated Children's Services*, Edinburgh: Scottish Executive

Scottish Executive (2002) *Assessing our Children's Educational Needs: The Way Forward? Scottish Executive Response to the Consultation*, Edinburgh: Scottish Executive

Scottish Executive (2003) *Report of the First Round of Accessibility Strategies*, Edinburgh: Scottish Executive

Scottish Executive (2005) *Supporting Children's Learning: Code of Practice*, Edinburgh: Scottish Executive

Scottish Executive (2006a) *Pupils in Scotland 2005*, Edinburgh: Scottish Executive

Scottish Executive (2006b) *Exclusions from Schools 2004/05*, Edinburgh: Scottish Executive

Scottish Office (1991 updated 1995) *The Parents' Charter for Scotland*, Edinburgh: The Scottish Office

Scottish Office (1993) *A Parents' Guide to Special Educational Needs*, Edinburgh: The Scottish Office

Scottish Office (1998) *Special Educational Needs in Scotland*, Edinburgh: The Scottish Office

Scottish Office Education Department (1987) *Curriculum and Assessment in Scotland: A Policy for the '90s*, Edinburgh: SOED

Scottish Office Education Department (1992a) *Better Information for Parents in Scotland* Edinburgh: SOED

Scottish Office Education Department (1992b) *Devolved School Management – Guidelines for Progress*, Edinburgh: SOED

Scottish Office Education Department (1993) *Special Educational Needs within the 5–14 Curriculum: Support for Learning*, Edinburgh: SOED

Scottish Office Education Department (1994) *Effective Provision for Special Educational Needs: A Report by HM Inspectors of Schools*, Edinburgh: SOED

Scottish Office Education and Industry Department (1996a) *Children and Young Persons with Special Educational Needs: Assessment and Recording* (Circular 4/96), Edinburgh: SOEID

Scottish Office Education and Industry Department (1996b) *How Good is Our School? Self-Evaluation Using Performance Indicators*, Edinburgh: SOEID

Scottish Office Education and Industry Department (1996c) *Improving Achievements in Scottish Schools: A Report to the Secretary of State for Scotland*, Edinburgh: SOEID

Scottish Office Education and Industry Department (1998a) *A Manual of Good Practice in Special Educational Needs*, Edinburgh: SOEID

Scottish Office Education and Industry Department (1998b) *Setting Targets – Raising Standards in Schools*, Edinburgh: SOEID

Scottish Office Education and Industry Department (1999a) *Targeting Excellence: Modernising Scotland's Schools*, Edinburgh: SOEID

Scottish Office Education and Industry Department (1999b) *Raising Standards – Setting Targets: Targets for Pupils with Special Educational Needs*, Edinburgh: SOEID

Scottish Parliament Education, Culture and Sports Committee (2001) *Report on the Inquiry into Special Educational Needs*, Edinburgh, Scottish Parliament

Special Educational Needs Tribunal (2000) *Special Educational Needs Tribunal: Annual Report 1999–2000*, London: The Stationery Office

Special Educational Needs and Disability Tribunal (2005) *Special Educational Needs and Disability Tribunal: Annual Report 2003–2004*, London: The Stationery Office

Stoll, L. (1991) 'School self-evaluation: another boring exercise or an opportunity for growth?', in Riddell, S. and Brown, S. (eds) (1991) *School Effectiveness Research: Its Messages for School Improvement*, Edinburgh: HMSO, pp. 47–57

Tisdall, K. and Riddell, S. (2006 forthcoming) 'Policies on school inclusion: competing strategies and discourses', *European Journal of Special Needs Education*

Tomlinson, J. (1997) 'Inclusive learning: the report of the committee of inquiry into the post-school education of those with learning difficulties and disabilities in England, 1996', *European Journal of Special Need Education*, Vol. 12, No. 3, pp. 184–96

Tomlinson, S. (1982) *A Sociology of Special Education*, London: Routledge and Kegan Paul

Vincent, C., Evans, J., Lunt, I. and Young, P. (1996) 'Professionals under pressure: the administration of special education in a changing context', *British Educational Research Journal*, Vol. 22, No. 4, pp. 475–90

Wearmouth, J. (ed.) (2001) *Special Educational Provision in the Context of Inclusion: Policy and Practice in Schools*, London: David Fulton Publishers in association with the Open University

Weatherley, R. and Lipsky, M. (1977) 'Street-level bureaucrats and institutional innovation: implementing special educational reform', *Harvard Educational Review*, Vol. 47, No. 2, pp. 171–97

Wolfendale, S. and Cook, G. (1997) *Evaluation of Special Educational Needs Parent Partnership Schemes*, London: DfEE

INDEX